The Institution of Lokpal in India

Exploring the Viability to Arrest Corruption

The Institution of Lokpal in India

Exploring the Viability to Arrest Corruption

Anil Kumar Vishwakarma

Foreword by

Hon'ble Justice Swatanter Kumar

(Former Judge Supreme Court of India)

Chairperson, National Green Tribunal (PB), New Delhi

GenNext Publication

ISBN : 978-93-8022-294-3

Price : ₹ 450

First Published, 2015

Published by

Gennext Publications
5, Ansari Road
Daryaganj, New Delhi-110002
Phones: 9811692060
E-mail: gennext@hotmail.com

Printed at: G. Print Process, Delhi.

Cataloging in Publication Data—DK
Courtesy: D.K. Agencies (P) Ltd. <docinfo@dkagencies.com>

Vishwakarma, Anil Kumar, author.
The institution of lokpal in India : exploring the viability to arrest corruption / Anil Kumar Vishwakarma (B.Sc, M.A, LL.B (D.U), LL.M (ILI)).
pages cm
Includes bibliographical references (pages).
ISBN 9789380222943

1. Ombudspersons—India. 2. Ombudspersons. 3. Corruption—Law and legislation—India. I. Title.

JQ229.O4V57 2016 DDC 352.350954 23

Contents

Justice Swatanter Kumar
Former Judge, Supreme Court of India
Chairperson, National Green Tribunal
New Delhi

Off. : Faridkot House,
Copernicus Marg, New Delhi-110 001
Ph. :011-23077937
Resi. : 9, Thyagraj Marg New Delhi 110011
Ph. : 011-23010300,23010039
email: ps.justsk@gmail.com

Foreword

Fairness and Transparency is of essence to the concept of constitutional governance. Corruption devalues human rights, chokes development and undermines justice, liberty, equality, fraternity which are the core values in our preambular vision. It is here the strong need for the institution which can effectively tackle the menace of corruption was felt.

In view of the diminishing values and uprightness it is necessary to provide uniform mechanism to attend to public grievances in relation to Government fuction. So the need of the institution like 'Ombudsman' was felt and the idea of the institution of Lokpal was borrowed from the concept of Ombudsman in countries such as Finland, Norway, Denmark, Sweden, U.K. and New Zealand. As a result India got the much awaited legislation 'The Lokpal and Lokayuktas Act, 2013' which received the assent of the President on the 1st January, 2014. The effectiveness and efficacy of these authorities dealing with corruption were in discussion on many occasions.

The author points out that the act is an anti-corruption law in India which seeks to provide for the establishment of the Institution of Lokpal and Lokayuktas to inquire into allegations of corruption against certain public functionaries. At present, agencies like Central Vigilance Commission, Central Bureau of Investigation and other similar bodies are involved in inquiring, investigating and prosecuting corruption cases. No doubt Lokpal work effectively, however proposition regarding the working of the Lokpal independently has always been a point of debate from the very beginning of the Lokpal and Lokayuktas Act, 2013.

Anil Kumar Vishwakarma, the author of this book titled "The Institution of Lokpal in India: Exploring the Viability to Arrest Corruption" is a teacher of law in the University of Delhi. He felt the need of looking in to the working of institution of Lokpal. He has made this attempt in that direction.

The attempt of the author is well directed and guided towards the working of the institution of Lokpal.

I appreciate the effort of the author and wish him the very best.

(Justice Swatanter Kumar)

New Delhi
7th October, 2015

Prologue:

The Inspiration

The seed for this book was sown the day I had joined the Faculty of Law, University of Delhi. It was in complete contrast between my upbringing in a very small place in Uttar Pradesh and the highly competetive environment of one of the best Law faculty in India. A will to bring about change keeping in mind the famous quote 'be the change you want to see in to the world' of Mahatma Gandhi, I thought of being a part of change.

Since my childhood, I grew older hearing a lot about First woman IPS officer, Kiran Bedi in serving the Nation. I would fail in my duty if I don't acknowledge the contribution she had made to my life. I remember a occasion of being in Jawahar Law Nehru University where she was invited to speak upon "Nation Building Projects" I had gone to get a glimpse of hers and was crying after getting my dream fulfilled.

I remember that it was my final year of LL.B. that Mr Arvind Kejriwal Ji had come to faculty of Law, University of Delhi and he spoke about problem of Corruption and urgent need of an independent mechanism to tackle the menace of corruption. It led to the formation of a group consisting of Kiran Bedi Mam, Kejriwal Ji and Anna Hazare Ji.

It was really very encouraging to see that whole national stood together and said it in one voice that 'together we can and we will'and asked for 'Jan Lokpal' which made the powerful realise the heat of 'we the people of India'.

I was associated with this movement from the very first dharna till the acceptance of the Lokpal. It was during my association with this movement which made me to give a serious thought to the importance of this institution.

This book is to acknowledge the efforts which people had made for demanding an independent investigating agency which does not seem to be fulfilled. We had demanded an agency which will be independent and free from any political intervention. Here I had made an effort to point out some areas of this much awaited legislation which requires a second thought.

With a lot of hope,

— Anil Kumar Vishwakarma

Acknowledgement

I take this opportunity to express my gratitude to Dr Manoj Kumar Sinha (Director, Indian Law Institue, New Delhi) for his endless emphasis on hard work and Dr Anurag Deep (Associate Professor, ILI) who kindly blessed me with his valuable suggestions at times to improve the work.

I am indebted to Dr Kiran Bedi, former IPS whose indefatigable spirit to serve the country and the movement 'India Against Corruption' for the Jan Lokpal Bill, germinated within me the seeds of inquisitiveness and inspired to come up with this book.

It is my divine obligation to ackowledge the contribution of my father Sri Ram Dularey and mother Smt Maha Rani, my sisters and brothers for an unparallel support in all respects.

Finally special thanks to my teachers The Rev. Rajendra Singh S/o Late. Goodwin Singh, Mr Vidhya Sagar Srivastava (Bhai Sahab), My friends Ram, Aslam, Atul, Vijay, Rais, Shailendra, Arun and all Indian Law Institute friends for their cooperation and encouragement.

This study bears testimony to the active contribution, and encouragement of a host of friends and well-wishers.

I dedicate this book and its proceeds to all those who stood together in a movement against corruption and showed that 'together we can and we will'.

List of Abbreviation

ACB	:	Anti Corruption Branch
AICC	:	All India Congress Committee
AIDS	:	Acquired Immune Deficiency Syndrome
AIR	:	All India Reporter
All LJ	:	Allahabad Law Journal
ARC	:	Administrative Reform Commission
ASILI	:	Annual Survey of Indian Law Institute
CJ.	:	Chief Justice
CAG	:	Comptroller and Auditor General
Cal.	:	Calcutta
CBI	:	Central Bureau of Investigation
CEC	:	Chief Election Commission
CEO	:	Chief Exective Officer
Cr.PC	:	Criminal Procedure Code
CVC	:	Central Vigilance Commission
DOPT	:	Department of Personnel and Training
DSPE	:	Delhi Special Police Establishment
Eg.	:	for Example
Ed.	:	Edition
IPC	:	Indian Penal Code

Ibid.	:	same as above
Id.	:	same as above different page
IPC	:	Indian Penal Code
JO	:	Justitie Ombudsman
JILI	:	Journal of Indian Law Institute
Ker.	:	Kerala
MLA	:	Member of Legislative Council
MP	:	Member of Parliament
MNREGA	:	Mahatma Gandhi National Rural Employment Guarantee Act
MO	:	Militie Ombudsman
NHRM	:	National Rural Health Mission
PM	:	Prime Minister
PMO	:	Prime Minister Office
SC	:	Supreme Court
SCC	:	Supreme Court Cases
SCJ	:	Supreme Court Journal
Supra	:	Written above
UK	:	United Kingdom
UPA	:	United Progressive Alliance
US	:	United States
USA	:	United States of America.

Chapter 1

Introduction

"Fearless investigation is a 'sine qua non' of exposure of delinquent 'greats' and if the investigative agencies tremble to probe or make public the felonies of high office, white collar offenders in the peaks may be unruffled by the law. An independent investigative agency to be set in motion by any responsible citizen is a desideratum"

Justice V.R. Krishna Iyer.[1]

1.1 Corruption : The Defitional Dilemma

Corruption is one of the important evils of the society whereby every human being gets himself affected by such evil practice by one or other.[2] Corruption in a civilised society is a disease like cancer, which if not detected in time is sure to malign the polity of country leading to disastrous consequences.[3] Its virus is compared with HIV leading to AIDS, being incurable, unless nipped in the bud at the earliest; it is likely to cause turbulence shaking off the socio-economic-political system in an otherwise healthy, wealthy, effective and vibrating society.[4] Corruption deepens poverty; it debases human rights, it degrades the environment; it derails development, including private sector development; it can drive conflict in and between nations; and it destroys confidence in democracy and the legitimacy of governments. It debases human dignity and is universally condemned by the worlds major faiths.[5] In *Dr. Subramanian Swamy* v. *Dr. Manmohan Singh*, [6] also the Supreme Court of India made following remarks:[7]

> Today, corruption in our country not only poses a grave danger to the concept of constitutional governance, it also threatens the very foundation of Indian democracy and the Rule of Law. The magnitude of corruption in our public life is incompatible with the concept of a socialist, secular democratic republic. It cannot be disputed that where corruption begins all rights end. Corruption devalues human rights, chokes development and undermines justice, liberty, equality, fraternity which are the core values in our preambular vision. Therefore, any anti-corruption law has to be interpreted and worked out in such a fashion as to strengthen the fight against corruption.[8]

This remark of the Supreme Court is an *obiter* mention but this is restatement of various topical issues involved in corruption in developing democracy like India.

In legal discourse the first important question is the definition. It has never been an easy task to define corruption because it is a blend of nature of a conduct viz moral, ethical, social, legal etc. Corruption is defined by the World Bank and Transparency International as "the misuse of public office for private gain."[9] It involves the improper and unlawful behaviour of public-service officials, both politicians and civil servants, whose positions create opportunities for the diversion of money and assets from the government to them and their accomplices.[10]

According to Transparency International, India was ranked among the world's highly corrupt nations at the 94th out of 177 countries spot in a global list of corruption perception index 2013.[11] According to the list, India has scored 36 points on a scale of 0-100, where 0 means that a country is perceived as highly corrupt and 100 means it is perceived as very clean.[12] India's rank has remained unchanged from the last year, It has emerged as more corrupt than three of its BRICS[13] peers-China (80th), South Africa and Brazil (both ranked 72nd).[14] Though the report of Transperency International is not a conclusive report but it definately is global indicator of how long India has to travel to check corruption and deliver good governance.

According to the Comptroller and Auditor General of India's report on the issue of corruption in Licences and Allocation of 2G Spectrum, there was a presumptive loss of Rs. 1766 billion (US$ 29 billion) by the United Progressive Alliance, UPA Government.[15]

To address the issue of corruption, three main authorities involved in inquiring, investigating and prosecuting corruption cases are the—

i. Central Vigilance Commission (CVC),
ii. Central Bureau of Investigation (CBI) and
iii. State Anti-Corruption Bureau (ACB).

Cases related to money laundering by public servants are investigated and prosecuted by the Directorate of Enforcement and the Financial Intelligence Unit, which are under the Ministry of Finance.

The effectiveness and efficacy of these authorities dealing with corruption were in discussion on many occasions. For addressing the issue of corruption the author has shown some data on the existing systems of identifying and prosecuting cases of corruption against public officials. Here is the Corruption cases data against government official.The government has frequently delayed sanction for prosecuting officials, so here is the data showing requests for prosecution sanction pending with the government (December, 2010).[16]

The Central government is less culpable in encouraging corruption because while around 30 per cent plus cases of corruption in Central government were granted decision on sanction in less than three months, State Government could take decision in 20 per cent cases.[17] But for cases around 40 per cent and above both are equally reluctant to decide.[18] The Central Vigilance Commission (CVC) is the premier agency tasked to tackle corruption cases within the Central government. The author found the same problem while observing the penalties imposed in pursuance of the Central Vigilance Commission's advice.

Penalties imposed in pursuance of Central Vigilance Commission's advice[19]

The Data shows that only 6 per cent of the cases were taken up for Prosecution and 94 per cent were given departmental penalties.[20]

i. Between the period from 2005 and 2009, penalties were imposed on 13, 061 cases (average 2612 per year) based on the CVC's advice.[21]

ii. This included 846 cases (annual average 169) in which sanction were granted for criminal prosecution.[22]

iii. Major penalties were imposed in 4895 cases (annual average 979). These include dismissal, reduction to lower rank, cut in pension etc.[23]

iv. Minor penalties such as censure were imposed on 5356 cases (annual average 1071), and administrative action was taken in 1964 cases (annual average 393).[24]

Number of complaints received by CVC[25]

i. The Supreme Court directed the government in 2004 to put a mechanism to act on the complaints which have been received from the whistleblowers.[26]

ii. In April 2004, the government passed a resolution with the object of empowering the Central Vigilance Commission to act on complaints from whistleblowers.[27]

iii. In the five years from 2005 to 2009, the CVC received a total of 1, 731 complaints, or an annual average of 346.[28]

Pendency of Central Bureau of Investigation (CBI) cases in the Courts[29]

The Central Bureau of Investigation is vested with task of handling the Corruption cases against the public officials effectively however the following data shows the CBI cases being in pendency for a long period. The criminal justice system has also been slow in prosecuting the CBI cases.[30]

i. By the end of 2010, there were 9, 927 CBI cases pending in courts.[31]

ii. And out of 2, 245 cases (23 per cent of the total) were pending for more than 10 years.[32]

The Central Vigilance Commission's functions are advisory.[33] The working of the C.B.I. independently, was questioned oftenly. Taking exception to the C.B.I. sharing its progress report on 'Coalgate scam' with the Law Minister and Joint Secretariess in the Prime Minister's office and Department of coal the Supreme Court characterised the CBI as 'a caged parrot speaking its masters' voice- "one parrot with many masters".[34] The constituionality of the institution of the CBI was also challenged in the high court of Guwahati.[35]

Millions of administrative decisions are made each year. Some of these decisions have been arbitrary or unjustified. As a result the magnitude of the citizen's grievances against administration has increased. But there is no effective machinery to get them redressed. The courts can provide rederess only in a limited way. Corruption and maladministration are closely interrelated. It may be necessary to have a unified machinery to deal with complaints in both these areas by machinery which will be independent of the executive branch of the Government for redressal of citizen's grievances. So the need of the institution like 'Ombudsman' was felt and the idea of the institution of Lokpal was borrowed from the concept of Ombudsman in countries such as Finland, Norway,

Denmark, Sweden, U.K. and New Zealand. It is now desirable to know the exact meaning of Ombudsman.

1.2 Ombudsman : Dictionary Meaning

The word 'Ombudsman' has got following meanings-

1.2.1 Black's Law Dictionary

Means an official appointed to receive, investigate, and report on private citizens' complaints about the government.[36]

1.2.2 Collins Dictionary of the English Language

1. A commissioner who acts as independent referee between individual citizens and their government or its administration. 2. (In Britain) an official, without power of sanction or mechanism of appeal, who investigates complaints of maladministration by members of the public against national or local government or its servants.[37]

1.2.3 Advanced Law Lexicon

An authority established either by the company or the Government for the quick redressal of grievances.[38] A popular name (derived from Sweden) for an official appointment to receive and investigate the complaints of citizens about the government and its officials.[39]

1.2.4 The Macquarie Dictionary

An official appointed by Parliament, or some other Legislative body, as a city council, to investigate complaints by citizens against the government or its agencies.[Swed.: commissioner][40]

1.2.5 Webster's Ninth New Collegiate Dictionary

1. A government official (as in Sweden or New Zealand) appointed to receive and investigate complaints made by individuals against abuses or capricious acts of public officials. 2. one that investigates reported complaints (as from students or

consumers), report's findings, and help to achieve equitable settlements.[41]

A person appointed by Parliament to investigate citizen's complaints of executive or bureaucratic incompetence or injustice, but not illegality. The first such officer was appointed in Sweden in 1809-10 with wide powers of enquiry. The institution was adopted in other Scandinavian countries—by Finland (1919), Denmark (1954), and Norway(1962). He is an independent investigator and must act impartially between the government and individual, but the scope of his investigations usually excludes legislative and judicial conduct.[42]

1.2.6 Ombudsman and Lokpal: The Difference

India does not use the word ombudsman but Lokpal. The author tried to find out the meaning of the word "Lokpal' which has not been defined in any of the above mentioned dictionaries, because of obvious reasons that the word Lokpal is of Indian origin. However the word "Ombudsman" has been used in India by various agencies viz Bank, insurance committee, media etc. it is also acknowledged in the University Grants Commission Gazette[43] and the word has been further described in Section 4 of the said Gazette.[44]

1.3 Ombudsman: Legal Meaning

In Swedish language the word 'Ombudsman' is derived from the Swedish word "Ombud" which means "a person who acts as a spokesman or representative of another person or persons."[45] In United States, the word 'Ombudsman' refers to a complaint handling mechanism.[46]

The Ombudsman Committee of the International Bar Association has suggested to refer the term to those grievance handling mechanisms which come within the scope of the following definition;

> An Ombudsman institution is an office for by the constitution or by action of the legislative or Parliament and headed by an independent, high level public official who is responsible to the legislative or Parliament, who receives complaints from aggrieved persons against government agencies, officials, and employees or who acts on his own motion and who has the power to investigate, recommend corrective action and issue reports.[47]

According to Caiden, the Ombudsman is “an institutionalised public conscience- the essence of what governments ought to do; that is to cultivate the well being of the Citizen, the preservation of individual liberty and the equitable treatment of all citizens by the public bureaucracy”.[48]

1.4 Where did it (Ombudsman) originate?

The Swedish Constitution provided for a unique institution called “Ombudsman” to control and check public authorities exercising powers of the states. The Institution of Ombudsman originated in Sweden in 1809.[49] It took over a century to spread to other countries-Finland in 1919, Denmark in 1955, West Germany in 1957, and Norway in 1961.[50]A modified version of the Ombudsman that is the office of the Parliamentary Commissioner was established in New Zealand in 1962 and in the United Kingdom in 1967.[51] The new New Zealand statute provided the model for the establishment of Ombudsman in Australia, Western Australia appointed an Ombudsman in 1971, South Australia in 1972, Victoria in 1973, Queensland in 1974, and New South Wales in 1975. Developments in United States began two years earlier than in Australia.[52] Hawaii was the first State to set up an Ombudsman in 1969, Nebraska appointed in 1971, Iowa in 1972, and Alaska in 1975, West Germany has had an Ombudsman of the Armed forces since 1957.Tanzania in 1966, Guyana in 1967, Mauritius in 1970, Fiji in 1972, Zambia in 1973.[53]

Table – 1. Year of the Introduction of the Institution of 'Ombudsman' in different Countries

Country	*Year of the Introduction of the Institution of 'Ombudsman'*
Sweden	1809
Finland	1919
Denmark	1955
West Germany	1957
Norway	1961
New Zealand	1962
United Kingdom	1967
West Australia	1971
South Australia	1972
West Germany	1957
Tanzania	1966
Guyana	1967
Mauritius	1970
Fizi	1972
Zambia	1973
India	2013

The above mentioned table brings into our knowledge that the Ombudsman institution emerged into the 19th Century and further with its successful address of the issue of corruption it was evolved by the developed and some of the developing countries in the 20th Centuary, however the office of Ombudsman got its existence in India during 21st Century. Since India is the 2nd largest country of the world, the author wishes to know, Do we really need the institution of ombudsman in India?, which will successfully address the issues of the citizens's against the corrupt public officers.

1.5 Why Ombudsman in India?

In any democratic set-up, such as ours, the citizens in theory are the masters and the government officials their servants. Theories on which government works must be tested in homes and market places, and not only in the conferences of specialists. If the Government is not run for the benefit of the common man and he loses faith in it is a failure.[54]

But in actual practise the concept appears to operate in the reverse order. While a government official enjoys certain powers vested in him as a trustee, holding a public office to act according to due process of law on behalf of the citizens collectively, the individual citizen suffers in practice from the ignorance and appears too weak before the government officials.[55]

The right to complain, the right to be heard, and the right to have corrective action taken if one has suffered harm from government are human rights.[56] Human rights are protected by effective machinery which implements the constitution, the law or the charter. The ombudsman is one of the institutions essential to a society under the Rule of law, a society in which fundamental rights and human dignity are respected.[57] Reasons for the desirability of the Ombudsman institution are as follows:

i. Extensive powers and discretion have been granted to all types of boards, agencies and departments of the Governments, capable of affecting the lives of everyone. The possibilities of friction between officials and the citizens have been greatly increased. Protection of the individual is required against executive and administrative mistake and abuse of power.[58]

ii. The existing mechanisms for adjusting grievances are inadequate.

iii. The legislator if starts investigating complaints is taken away from his main function of studying and passing legislation.[59] He must of necessity rely in most cases upon a reply from the agency or department he is investigating. Partly affiliation may affect his role in handling grievances. In Parliamentary countries like ours, the investigation is by the department against whom the complaint has been made.[60]

iv. The courts play a major role in the correction of abuses by the government. But litigation is expensive, dilatory and in many cases, the citizen bears with injustice because he can not afford litigation.[61]

v. Administrative courts even when using procedures as informal as possible still follow court like adversary procedure. Such courts usually move slowly and there is great delay in ensuring the execution of the judgement when delivered.[62]

vi. Executive complaint agencies lack the essential characteristics of independence from the executive.

vii. Administrative agencies may have within their structure channels for complaints but such system lacks impartiality. The appeal system, if one exists, is expensive and time – consuming.

In view of the failure of to meet the maladministration, the institution of the Ombudsman was explored which may investigate into complaint of corrupt practices, undue delay and misuse of powers independently of the executive branch of government.[63] Santhanam Committee observed: "it is now an agreed fact that the prevailing corruption in the country is the ulcer in the stomach of India' administration."[64] This acknowledgement shows that India was concerned for this menace of corruption in the decades of 60 and it was this decade in which Ombudsman found its first significant introduction but with inconsistent approach of parliament.

1.6 Lokpal : The Struggle for Existence

The idea of the Ombudsman was first talked by late Mr K.M. Munshi, who was a member of the constituent assembly of India in 1960. He decried the idea of setting up of such a tribunal and instead commended the Swedish practice regarding appointment of an ombudsman for controlling maladministration.[65]

On the 3rd April, 1963, while the demands for the grants of the Law Ministry were being debated, Dr L.M. Singhvi, M.P., raised the issue of setting up an institution of ombudsman in very emphatic terms and consistently campaigned for it in the Parliament during the years 1963 to 1965.[66] On the 3rd November, 1963 late Pundit Nehru, the then Prime Minister of India, in his address to the All- India Congress Committee (AICC), at Jaipur admitted that the ombudsman's idea had fascinated him, for the official had the overall authority to deal with the charges even against the Prime Minister and commanded respect and confidence of all. He, however, felt that in a big country like India, it was be set with difficulties.[67] On the 9th April, 1965 a resolution was moved in the Lok Sabha (House of the People) for setting up a committee of the Members of the Parliament to examine the question of suitable machinery for the redress of citizen's grievances including the institution of the ombudsman.[68]

In its interim report on the "Problems of Redressal of Citizens' grievances" submitted in 1996, the Administrative Reforms Commission recommended the setting up of an institution of Lokpal at the centre.[69] The Lokpal Bill was introduced for the first time in 1968 but it lapsed with the dissolution of the Lok sabha. To give effect to the recommendations of the administrative Reforms Commission, eight bills on Lokpal were introduced in the Lok Sabha in 1971, 1977, 1985, 1989, 1995, 2001, 2005 and 2008 to the past but no Central legislation was passed. So far 18 states have created the institution of the Lokayukta through the Lokayukta Acts.[70]

The Second Administrative Commission, formed in 2005, also recommended that the office of the Lokpal be established without delay. In January 2011, the Government formed a Group of minsters, Chaired by Shri Pranab Mukherji to suggest measures to tackle corruption, including examination of the proposal of a Lokpal Bill.[71]

In order to draw the attention of the government to such burning issue, a campaign "India against corruption" was started by Anna Hazare for the demand of strong anti corruption "Jan Lokpal Bill" in 2011. This movement got momentum and led the Government to feel the heat of it.

The government has issued a gazette notification for setting up a joint committee consisting of 10 members from the government as well as the civil society to draft the Lokpal Bill. The drafting committee was officially formed on 8 April 2011. The Government of India accepted that the committee be co-chaired by a politician and an activist, non-politician. It is reported that Pranab Mukherjee, from the political arena and Shanti Bhusan, from civil society will fill those roles.

In 2011, during the winter session of the Parliament, the Lok Sabha passed the controversial Lokpal bill but couldn't be passed by the Rajya Sabha due to shortage of time in winter session of 2011. The government put the Lokpal Bill in the Rajya Sabha on 13th December 2013 and was adjourned till 16th December 2013 in want of debate. The Bill (The Lokpal and Lokayuktas Act, 2013) was passed in the Rajya Sabha on 17th December, 2013 after making certain amendments to the earlier Bill and in the Lok Sabha on 18th December, 2013.[72] The Lokpal and Lokayuktas Act, 2013 received the assent of the President on the 1st January, 2014.

The Act is an anti-corruption law in India which seeks to provide for the establishment of the Institution of Lokpal and Lokayuktas to inquire into allegations of corruption against certain public functionaries and for matters connecting them but India had agencies like Central Vigilance Commission, and Central Bureau of Investigation authorities involved in inquiring, investigating and prosecuting corruption cases in such a situation, will the Lokpal work effectively, however proposition regarding the working of the Lokpal independently has always been a point of debate from the very beginning of the Lokpal and Lokayuktas Act, 2013. From the Appointment of the Selection Committee to the Search Committee, there have been controversies after the Lokpal and Lokayuktas Act, 2013 came into force. The Search Commttee Rules 2014 does not apppear in consonance with 'The Lokpal and Lokayuktas Act, 2013' which will lead to defeat the very purpose of the institution of the Lokpal.

The author has tried to find out whether the introduction of the Institution of the Lokpal under the new legislation of 'The Lokpal and Lokayuktas Act, 2013' will prove to be the prime institution in the field of investigation and tackling the menace of corruption and at the same time it will not subject to corruption and act independently. He has also tried to find out the issues which may come across while implementing the provisions of the Lokpal and Lokayuktas Act, 2013. Looking at the importance of the institution, It is equally desirable to see how this institution has developed.

References

1. *In Re The Special Courts Bill*, 1978 1 SCC 380, at p. 466, at para 126.
2. Dr P.C. Pati, "Corruption in India : Measures for its Prevention with reference to Prevention of Corruption Act, 1988" Vol XXXI (3&4) *Indian Bar Review* 349 (2004).
3. *Ibid.*
4. *State of Madhya Pradesh* v. *Shri. Ram Singh,* AIR 2000 SCC 870 at para 7.
5. C. Raj Kumar, *Corruption and Human Rights in India* 1 (Oxford University Press, New Delhi, 2011).
6. AIR 2012 SC 1185: decided on 31 Jan. 2012, hereinafter referred as *Dr Swamy*. The unanimous decision has been given by division bench of G. S. Singhvi and Asok Kumar Ganguly JJ. However, two separate judgements were delivered.
7. *Id.* para 11.
8. Anurag Deep, "Interpretation of statutes" XLVIII, *ASIL*573-74(2012).
9. Chandra Shekhar Joshi, "Need of Lokpal as Legal Instrument for Prevention of Corruption in India"48, *Civil and Military Law Journal* 93 (2012).
10. *Ibid.*

11. Corruption Perception Index, India, *available at: http://www.transparency.org/country#IND (Visited* on February 01, 2014).
12. *Ibid.*
13. BRICS stands for Brazil Russia India China South Africa, which is a group of five major emerging national economies.
14. *Ibid.*
15. Comptroller and Auditor General of India, *Report on Performance Audit on the issue of Licences and Allocation of 2G Spectrum*, (March, 2010).
16. Corruption cases against government officials, Requests for prosecution sanction pending with the government (Dec, 2010), India, *available at: http://www.prsindia.org/administrator/uploads/general/1302269425~~Vital%20Stats%20-% 20 Corruption % 20 cases % 20 against % 20 government % 20 officials % 2008 Apr 11. pdf* (Visited on February 13, 2014).
17. *Ibid.*
18. *Ibid.*
19. Corruption cases against government officials, Penalties imposed (in pursuance of CVC's advice), India, *available at: http://www.prsindia.org/administrator/uploads/general/1302269425~~Vital%20Stats%20-% 20 Corruption % 20 cases % 20 against % 20 government % 20 officials % 2008 Apr 11. pdf* (Visited on February 13, 2014).
20. *Ibid.*
21. *Ibid.*
22. *Ibid.*
23. *Ibid.*
24. *Ibid.*
25. Corruption cases against government officials, Number of Complaints received by CVC, India, *available at: http://www.prsindia.org/administrator/uploads/general/1302269425~~Vital%20Stats%20-%20Corruption%20cases%20against%20government%20officials%2008Apr11.pdf(Visited* on February 13, 2014).
26. *Ibid.*
27. *Ibid..*
28. *Ibid.*
29. Corruption cases against government officials, The courts have been slow in deciding CBI cases, India, *available at: http://www.prsindia.org/administrator/uploads/general/1302269425~~Vital%20Stats%20-*

%20Corruption%20cases%20against%20government%20officials%2008Apr11.pdf (Visited on February 13, 2014).

30. *Ibid.*
31. *Ibid.*
32. *Ibid.*
33. Joseph Ponnoly, "Dealing with maladministration- The need for ombudsman in India", *C.B.I. Bulletin* 26 (1996).
34. Dr P.R. Dubhashi, "Independence of the CBI, police and Administration", *Mainstream 19* (2013).
35. *Navendra Kumar* v. *Union of India & Another*, High Court of Guwahati, 2013.
36. *Black's Law Dictionary*, 7th Edn., p.1115.
37. *Collins Dictionary of the English Language*. Patrick Hanks (Editor), Wm. Collins Publishers Pvt. Ltd. 1986, Sydney, 2nd Ednq.
38. *Advanced Law Lexicon*, 3rd Edn., p. 3331.
39. *Ibid.*
40. *The Macquarie Dictionary*, 1st Edn., p.1208.
41. *Webster's Ninth New Collegiate Dictionary*, 9th Edn., 823.
42. *The Oxford Companion to Law Dictionary,* 903.
43. Section 2(k) as "Ombudsman" means the ombudsman appointed under the regulation 4 of the regulations of the University Grant Commission, the gazette of India, March 23, 2013 (CHAITRA 2, 1935).
44. Section 4(2) The Ombudsman shall be a person who has been a Judge not below the rank of a District Judge or a retired professor who has at least ten years' experience as a professor.
45. Girdhar B. Sharma, *Implementation of Ombudsman Plan In India* 6 (Ashish Publishing House, New Delhi, 1981).
46. Bernard Frank, "The Ombudsman Revisited", *International Bar Journal* 55(1975).
47. *Ibid.*
48. Norman Lewis and S.S. Singh "Citizen, Administration, and Ombudsman" in Norman Lewis, S.S Singh et.el. (eds), *Ombudsman India and The World Community, 2* (1995).
49. R.K. Dhawan, "*Public Grievances and the Lokpal*" 165 (Allied Publishers Private Limited, New Delhi, 1st edn., 1981).
50. *Ibid.*
51. *Ibid.*
52. *Ibid.*

53. *Ibid.*
54. M. Hidayatullah, "*Democracy in India and the Judicial Process*" 25 (Asia Publishing House, 1966).
55. Jagannadham and Makhija, "*Citizen's Administration and Lokpal*" 9 (S. Chand & Co., 1969).
56. Girdhar B. Sharma, "*Implementation of Ombudsman Plan In India*", 13 (Ashish Publishing House, New Delhi, 1981).
57. *Ibid.*
58. *Ibid.*
59. *Ibid.*
60. *Ibid.*
61. *Ibid.*
62. *Ibid.*
63. D.R. Saxena, *Ombudsman(Lokpal): Redress of citizens in India, 22* (Deep and Deep, New Delhi, 1987).
64. Government of India, Report: *Committee on Prevention of Corruption,* (Ministry of Law and Justice, 1964).
65. R.K. Swamy, "*The case for a Permanent Tribunal of Inquiry*", Modern Review, 264, 1964.
66. M.C.J. Kargi, "Control of the Administration" 254-55 *Public Law Journal*, (1968).
67. Girdhar B. Sharma, "*Implementation of Ombudsman Plan In India*", 25 (Ashish Publishing House, New Delhi, 1981).
68. *Ibid.*
69. *Ibid.*
70. *Ibid.*
71. *Ibid.*
72. Lokpal and Lokayukta Act, 2013.

Chapter 2

Historical Development of the Institution of Ombudsman

The pressure for rapid development implies that individual rights and the fine points of fair legal procedures are more likely to be disregarded in the interests of speed, efficiency and the broader public interest. Also the bureaucrats in many former colonies have inherited from their colonial masters an attitude of superiority, rather than service, an insolence of office which often leads to arbitrariness.[1]

2.1 Ombudsman : Origin

The word "Ombudsman, " now constituting an integral part of the English language, is derived from the Swedish word "Ombud" which in Swedish language commonly denotes "a person who acts as a spokesman or representative of another person or persons."[2] However, the word "ombudsman" lately started to be referred to a mechanism for handling complaints whether governmental or non- governmental, more particularly in the United States.[3]

An effort has been made to standardise the meaning of the term ombudsman. Stressing the need for uniformity in the use of the term ombudsman, the ombudsman Committee of the

International Bar Association has suggested that the term be employed only to refer to those grievances handling mechanisms which come within the scope of the following definition:

> An Ombudsman institution is an office for by the constitution or by action of the legislative or Parliament and headed by an independent, high level public official who is responsible to the legislative or Parliament, who receives complaints from aggrieved persons against government agencies, officials, and employees or who acts on his own motion and who has the power to investigate, recommend corrective action and issue reports.[4]

This definition is limited because it uses 'aggrived persons' to complain.Therefore a public spirited person, media etc. cannot complain.

2.2 Ombudsman : Development as Institution

The Swedish Constitution of 1809 provided for a unique institution called "Ombudsman" to control and check public authorities exercising powers of the states.[5] Following the Swedish example, the institution of the Parliamentary Ombudsman was included in the Constitution Act of 1919[6]. After ombudsman's adoption by Finland, Norway, another Scandinavian country set-up an ombudsman scheme for in 1963.[7] In 1955 Denmark's first ombudsman took office and began to function.[8] Norway appointed an ombudsman for civil affairs in 1962. In the same year New Zealand became the first country in the Commonwealth too adopt the ombudsman institution.

Since 1962 such institutions have been set up in a large number of countries and in great many there is a move to set-up similar type of institutions. England is a country with a parliamentary system to adopt the system of the ombudsman in 1966.[9]

In the following countries ombudsman or ombudsman like institutions have already been established at one or the other levels of government and are presently in operation: Australia; Austria, Canada; Official Languages Commissioner at the federal level, Fiji, France, Great Britain, Guyana, India (Commission for scheduled Castes and Scheduled Tribes, Minorities Commission at the Federal level and Lokayuktas in the states of Bihar, Maharashtra, Rajasthan, and Uttar Pradesh).[10] Israel (Commissioner for complaints from public, Soldiers' Complaint Commissioner, Commissioner for the city of Jerusalem, and Cities of Tel Aviv and Haifa); Italy (Region of Tuscany); Mauricious, Northern Ireland (Parliamentary Commissioner for Administration; and Commissioner for Complaints); Papua New Guinea (Ombudsman type 3 commission); Switzerland (city of Zurich); Tanzania and Zambia. In the United States there are ombudsman officials in the some of the states.[11]

The Ombudsman system existed in as many as 25 countries by 1977. Besides in countries like Bangladesh, Philippines and Greece, provisions pertaining to the establishment of ombudsman–like institutions have been incorporated in their respective constitutions but no enabling laws have been yet enacted.[12] The purpose of this entire ombudsman is to keep an eye on corrupt practices and check the menace of corruption by legal means.

2.3 Ombudsman : One Mechanism to Check Corruption

The basic idea of the institution of Lokpal was borrowed from the concept of Ombudsman in countries such as Finland, Norway, Denmark, Sweden, U.K., and New Zealand in 1809.[13] In 1995, the European Union created the post of European Ombudsman. Currently around 140 countries have the office of the Ombudsman.[14]

Ombudsman is an official, independent of the administration with power to investigate the citizen's complaints of maladministration.[15] The notion of maladministration incorporates any complaint tainted with (a) nepotism, corruption or bias; (b) failure to observe a sound administrative basis; (c) negligence in carrying out a duty; (d) misuse of discretion; (e) incompetence; and (f) tardiness and delay.

He is mostly free to choose his investigation and method and agency.[16] The expenditure of the office is under Parliamentary control. In Sweden, Denmark and Finland, the office of the Ombudsman can address complaints from the public or suo moto.[17]

However, in the case of the U.K. the office of the Parliamentary Commissioner can receive complaints only through Members of Parliament.[18] Sweden and Finland also have the power to prosecute erring public servants. Inspired by the suceess of the Ombudsman abroad, the idea of the grievance handling mechanism got its origin in India.

2.4 Origin and Development of Lokpal in India

The concept of ombudsman is not new idea for the Indians. It was first talked of in the country by late Mr K.M.Munsi, a constitutional pundit, a parliamentarian and a novelist who was also the member of the constituent assembly of India in February, 1960, i.e., at least two years before its introduction in the New Zealand.[19] Participating in the national debate on the need for the permanent Tribunal of Inquiry, in a statement to the press, he mooted the idea of setting up of such a tribunal and instead commended the Swedish practice regarding appointment of an ombudsman for controlling maladministration.[20]

The Credit for generating a live interest and debate on the ombudsman goes to late Mr M.C. Setalvad, the then Attorney General of India, who in the course of his inaugural address to the Third All-India Law Conference in the August, 1962 (New Delhi) urged upon the participants to undertake a study about its feasibility in India.[21] Again on 9th October, 1962 during his lecture to the public service probationers at the National Academy of Administration, Mr Setalvad reiterated the need for an expert body to study the body the implications of the adoption of such an institution by India.[22]

On April 3, 1963[23] when the demands for the grants of Law Ministry were being debated in Lok Sabha, Dr L.M. Singhvi stressed the need for the setting up of an ombudsman institution.[24] In July 1963, Mr P.B. Gajendragadkar, C.J. of the Supreme Court of India, in his address to the members of the Indian Institute of Public Administration commending the ombudsman idea, made a very strong plea for its adoption by India.[25]

Officially, the institution of such kind was first spoken of in India by the Rajasthan Administrative Reforms Committee. In their report submitted to the state Government in September, 1963, the Committee strongly recommended the appointment of an Ombudsman for the state.[26] On the 3rd November, 1963 late Pundit Nehru, the then Prime Minister of India, in his address to the All-India Congress Committee (AICC), at Jaipur admitted that the ombudsman's idea had fascinated him, for the official had the overall authority to deal with the charges even against the Prime Minister and commanded respect and confidence of all. He however, felt that in a big country like India, it was beset with difficulties.[27]

A resolution was moved in the House of the People On the 9th April, 1965 for setting up a committee of the Members of the Parliament to examine the question of a suitable machinery for the redress of citizen's grievances including the institution of the ombudsman.[28] The then Minister of State in the Ministry of Home Affairs referred to the fact that a Study Group of Members of both the Houses was already working on the task of administrative reforms and requested that its report to be awaited.[29]

Before the said Study Group of M.P's could come out with its report, the Government of India decided to appoint a high powered "Hoover-type" Administrative Reforms Commission in January 1966 and assigned to it inter alia the task of considering the problems of redress of citizens' grievances.[30]

2.5 Key Recommendations of Commissions

A number of commissions had made recommendations on various aspects of the office of Lokpal including procedure of appointment, powers of inquiry, and powers of prosecution.

2.5.1 Administrative Reform Commissions (ARC)

In its report dated the 20th October, 1966, the Administrative Reforms Commission, has advocated the adoption of the ombudsman – type institution for redress of citizen's grievances.[31]

The redress of citizen's grievances, the commission feels, is basic to the functioning of democratic governments, and will strengthen the hands of the government in administering the laws of the land, its policies "without fear or favour", enable it to go up in favour of the public faith and confidence in absence of which progress would not be possible.[32]

It had emphasised the view that such an institution would prove to be of immense and lasting utility "for the removal of a prevailing or lingering sense of injustice springing from administrative act which is the sine qua non of a popular administration."[33]

In suggesting the Scheme, the commission has taken note of the one side of the feeling of the public against the prevailing corruption, widespread inefficiency and administration's unresponsiveness to popular needs and on the other side to give protection to the administration to project its image and to dispel from the minds of the public false notions and prejudices against the quality and character of the administration.[34]

The main issue before Commission was to provide the citizen with an institution to which he can have easy access for the redress of his grievances which he is unable to seek elsewhere. The individual himself has the feeling of grievance whatever the nature of the grievance may be and it is for the state to try every method to restore the public' faith in to the government.[35]

A reasonable opportunity of presenting his case before an authority which is in a different hierarchy from the authority which passes the order and which is independent and impartial, would in itself be a source of satisfaction to the citizen concerned even where the result of investigation is unfavourable to him.[36]

The need for ensuring the rectitude of the administrative machinery is not only obvious but paramount. A Forum where the citizen can establish the genuineness of his case, it is plainly the duty of the state to set right the wrong done to him. The need for giving this approach a concrete form arises from the fact parliamentary supervision by itself cannot fully ensure to the citizen that rectitude over the entire area covered by administrative discretion.[37]

The Commission has suggested that the special circumstances relating to India can be fully met by providing for two special institutions for the redress of citizen's grievances.[38] One of these may be designated as Lokpal and he should deal with complaints against administrative acts of Ministers or Secretaries to the Government at the Centre and in the States. There should be another authority in each state and at the Centre to be designated as Lokayukta for dealing with complaints against the administrative acts of other officials.[39]

The Commission sought to achieve the following objectives-[40]

These officers should be demonstrably independent of the executive, legislature and the judiciary and be impartial—

i. Their investigations and proceedings should be conducted in private and should be informal in character, that their appointment, as far as possible should be non-political,
ii. That their status should compare with the highest judicial functionaries in the country;

iii. That they should deal with matters in the discretionary field involving acts of injustice, corruption or favouritism;

iv. That their proceedings should not be subject to judicial interference and they should have the maximum latitude and powers in obtaining information relevant to their duties;

v. That they should not look forward to any benefit or pecuniary advantage from the executive government.[41]

vi. The Lokpal had within his purview investigation of complaints against the Ministers and Secretaries, both at the Centre and in the States. The Lokpal should be appointed by the President on the advice of the Prime Minister which would be tendered by him after consultation with the Chief Justice of India and the Leader of the Opposition in the Lok Sabha.[42] If there is no such leader, Prime Minister will then consult a person elected by the members of the Opposition in the Lok Sabha in such manner as the Speaker may direct.

The salary and other emoluments of Lokpal will be the same as those of the Chief Justice of India. After his retirement from the position of the Lokpal, he will be ineligible for any appointment under the government (both Centre and State) or in a government Undertaking.[43] The Lokpal will be free to choose his own staff, but their number, categories and conditions of service will be subject to the approval of the President. His budget would be subject to the control of the Parliament.[44]

The Lokpal may in his discretion, inquire into a complaint of maladministration involving not only an act of injustice but also an allegation of favouritism to any person or of the accrual of personal benefit or gain to the administrative authority responsible for the act namely, a minister, or a Secretary to Government at the Centre or in the States.[45] In addition to making investigations on the basis of complaints received by him, the Lokpal may also *suo moto* investigate administrative acts which may come to his notice otherwise than through a complaint of an adversely affected person.

The following matters were to be excluded from the purview of the Lokpal:[46]

i. Action taken in a matter certified by a Minister as affecting the relations or dealings between the Government of India and any foreign Government or any international organisations of States or governments.[47]

ii. Action taken under the Extradition Act, 1962 or the Foreigners Act, 1946.

iii. Action taken for the purpose of investigation of crime or protecting the security of the State including action taken with respect to passports.[48]

iv. Action taken in the exercise of power in relation to determining whether a matter shall go to a court or not.[49]

v. Action taken in respect of appointments, removals, pay, superannuation or other personnel matters.[50]

vi. Any action in respect of which the person aggrieved has or had the right of appeal, reference or review to or before a tribunal constituted by or under any enactment.[51]

vii. Any administrative action which was taken more than twelve months before the date of the complaint.[52]

2.5.2 National Commission to review the working of the Constitution (2002)[53]

i. The Constitution should provide for the appointment of the Lok Pal. But the office of the Prime Minister should be kept out of the purview of the Lok Pal.

ii. Its finding should be final and form the basis for action by the government.

iii. The Constitution should make it obligatory for states to establish the institution of Lokayuktas.

iv. The Constitution should be amemded to state that Members of Parliament may be prosecuted for the offence of giving or receiving monetary or other valuable considerations for voting in a particular manner or not voting.

v. An MP can be prosecuted after the investigation agency receives prior sanction from a committee constituted by the President. The committee shall have five MPs, nominated by the President in consultation with the Speaker of the Lok Sabha and the Chairman of the Rajya Sabha.

2.5.3 Second Administrative Reform Commission (2007)[54]

Lokpal

i. The Constitution should be amended to provide for a national Ombudsman called the Rashtriya Lokayukta. The role and jurisdiction of the Rashtriya Lokayukta should be defined in the Constitution while the composition, mode of appointment and other details can be decided by Parliament through the legislation.[55]

ii. The Prime Minister should be kept out of the jurisdiction of the Rashtriya Lokayuktas.[56]

iii. I should consist of a serving or retired jugde of the Supreme Court as the Chairperson, an eminent jurist as Member and the Central Vigilance Commissioner as the ex-officio Member.[57]

iv. The Chairperson and members of the Rashtriya Lokayukta should be selected by a committee consisting of the Vice President, the Prime Minister, The Leader of the opposition, The speaker of the Lok Sabha and the Chief Justice of India.[58]

Lokayukta

i. The Constitution should make it obligatory on the part of the state governments to have Lokayuktas Institution.[59]

ii. The Lokayuktas should be a multi–member body consisting of a judicial Member if the Chair, an eminent jurist or eminent administrator as Member and the head of the State Vigilance Commission as ex- officio Member.[60]

iii. The Chairperson and member of the Lokayukta should be selected by a committee of the Chief Minister, Chief justice of the High court and the Leader of the Opposition in the Legislative Assembly.[61]

iv. The jurisdiction of the Lokayukta would extend to only cases involving corruption. They should not look into general public grievances. The Lokayukta should deal with cases of corruption against Ministers and MLAs.

v. Each State should constitute a State Vigilance Commission to look into cases of corruption against state government officials. The Commission should have three Members and have functions similar to that of the Central Vigilance Commission. The Anti Corruption Bureaus should be brought under the control of the State Vigilance Commission[62]

2.6 Investigation and Prosecution[63]

i. The State Vigilance Commissions and Lokayuktas should supervise the prosecution of corruption related cases.

ii. The investigative agencies should acquire multi-disciplinary skills and should be thoroughly conversant with the working of various departments. Modern techniques of investigation should be used such as electronic surveillance, video and audio recording of surprise inspections, traps, searches and seizures.[64]

iii. A reasonable time limit for investigation of different types of cases should be fixed for the investigative agencies.[65]

iv. There should be sustained step-up in the number of cases detected and investigated. The priorities need to be reoriented by focussing on 'big' cases of corruption.[66]

v. The prosecution of corruption cases should be conducted by a panel of lawyers prepared by the Attorney General or the Advocate General in consultation with Rashtriya Lokayukta or the Lokayukta.[67]

vi. The anti-corruption agencies should conduct surveys of departments with particular reference to highly corruption prone ones in order to gather intelligence and to target officers of questionable integrity.[68]

vii. The economic offences unit of states needs to be strengthened to effectively investigate cases and there should be better coordination among the existing agencies.[69]

The idea of Lokpal was borrowed from the office of the ombudsman which played an effective role in checking corruption and wrong –doing in Scandinavian countries (Sweden, Denmark, Finland, and Norway).The idea of constituting an Ombudsman type institution to look in the grievances of individuals against administration was first mooted in 1963 by late Mr L.M. Singhvi a member of Parliament during a debate.[70] Under the Chairmanship of Morarji Desai Commission was set up to investigate and recommend the concept of Ombudsman in India. In its interim report on the "Problems of Redressal of Citizens' grievances" submitted in 1996, the Administrative reforms Commission recommended the setting up of an institution of Lokpal at the centre.[71]

The Lokpal Bill was introduced for the first time in 1968 but lapsed. Later efforts were made to introduce the bill and eight bills were introduced in the Lok Sabha but it was not passed.[72] In 2002, the report of the National Commission to Review the working of the Constitution urged that the Constitution should provide for the appointment of the Lokpal and Lokayuktas in the states but suggested that the Prime minister should be kept out of the purview of the authority.[73] In 2004, the UPA government's National Common Minimum Programme promised that the Lokpal Bill would be enacted.[74] In 2005 The Second Administrative Commission, recommended that the office of the Lokpal be established without delay. Having a serious view of it, the Government formed a Group of ministers, Chaired by Shri Pranab Mukherji to suggest measures to tackle corruption, including examination of the proposal of a Lokpal Bill.

A campaign "India against corruption" was started by Anna Hazare for the demand of strong anti corruption "Jan Lokpal Bill" in 2011 which received a lot of support from the people and forced the government to view the issue of corruption seriously which led the government to issued a gazette notification for setting up a joint committee consisting of 10 members from the government as well as the civil society to draft the Lokpal Bill. The drafting committee was officially formed on 8 April 2011. The committee was chaired by that Pranab Mukherjee, from the political arena and Shanti Bhusan, from civil society.

In 2011, during the winter session of the Parliament, the Lok Sabha passed the controversial Lokpal bill but couldn't be passed by the Rajya sabha due to shortage of time in winter session of 2011. The government put the Lokpal Bill in the Rajya sabha on 13th December 2013 and was adjourned till 16th December 2013 in want of debate. The Bill (The Lokpal and Lokayuktas Act, 2013) was passed in the Rajya Sabha on 17th December, 2013 after making certain amendments to the earlier Bill and in the Lok Sabha on 18th December, 2013.[75] The author at the below mentioned table has discussed the development of the office of the Lokpal in India.

2.7 Table No. 2 A Brief Timeline of the Lok Pal Act.[76]

1960	The idea of the Ombudsman was first talked by late Mr K.M. Munshi, who was a member of the constituent assembly of India.
1963	It first came up in the Parliament during a discussion on the budget allocation for the Law Ministry.
1966	The first Administrative Reforms Commission recommended the setting up of two independent authorities-at the central and state level to look into the complaints against public functionaries, including MPs.
1968	The Lokpal bill was introduced before a Parliamentary committee for review. The committee decided to keep the prime minister out of the bill's purview.
1969	A revised version of the bill was introduced in the Lok Sabha. The lower house of Parliament passed the legislation. Rajya Sabha, the upper house, however, didn't take up the bill for discussion.
1971	The bill was again introduced in the Lok Sabha with minor changes. A few states had already implemented the Lokayuktas or watchdog bill at a state level. But yet again, the bill didn't manage to cross all hurdles before the session of the national Parliament ended.
2002	The Commission to review the working of the Constitution (Headed by Shri M.N Venkatachiliah) recommended the appointment of the Lokpal and Lokayuktas; also recommended that the PM be kept out of the ambit of the authority of The Lokpal.
2005	The Second Administrative Reforms Commission (Chaired by Shri Veerappa Moily) recommended that Office of the Lokpal be established without delay.
2011	The Government formed a Group of Ministers, chaired by Pranab Mukherjee to suggest measures to tackle corruption and examine the proposal of the Lokpal Bill.
1971-2011	The bill was re-introduced six times in the Parliament but wasn't passed because of lack of consensus. In 1989, the prime minister was brought under the bill's jurisdiction for the first time. Vishwanath Pratap Singh was the prime minister at the time.

April 2011	A month after meeting Prime Minister Manmohan Singh to discuss enlisting people from outside government to help draft a bill to set up an anti-corruption ombudsman's office, social activist and anticorruption crusader Anna Hazare began fasting at central Delhi's Jantar Mantar, a designated spot for political sit-ins and protests in the capital city. Mr Hazare's fast lasted for three days as the government decided to form a joint panel of ministers and civil society activists to draft the bill.
June 2011	The government and Mr Hazare's team failed to reach a consensus on the bill.
July 2011	The cabinet approved the draft bill which did not have jurisdiction over the prime minister.
August 4, 2011	The bill is introduced in the Lok Sabha amid widespread agitation by anticorruption protesters since the scope of the law did not extend to the prime minister.
August 16, 2011	Mr Hazare was arrested and sent to Tihar Jail under a temporary legal provision that banned public gatherings and protests at a New Delhi park where he was planning to hold his hunger strike .
August 19, 2011	Mr Hazare was released from prison after agreeing with the government's demand to hold a protest for only two weeks and headed straight to Ramlila ground, a vast public ground in the heart of Delhi where he launched his hunger strike.
August 29, 2011	Mr Hazare ended his 13-day hunger strike after India's Parliament adopted a resolution agreeing to so-called Team Anna's key demands for a bill to set up an independent anticorruption agency.
December 20, 2011	India's Cabinet had approved its own version of the bill. But Mr Hazare and his aides remained unhappy with the government's version, which failed to meet his key demands.
December 23, 2011	India's government introduced the legislation in Parliament, amid protests from opposition parties and anticorruption activists, setting the stage for another showdown in the legislature.

December 27, 2011	The Lokpal and Lokayuktas Bill were passed by the Lok Sabha. The bill was tabled a week before on December 22. However, Rajya Sabha opposed to the bill during the session.
September, 2012	The bill was shortlisted for consideration and passing after the approval of the Rajya Sabha's select committee, a body of lawmakers appointed to review and amend proposed legislation, during the monsoon session that started August 8. Lawmakers failed to pass it.
December, 2012	The proposed anticorruption law was again on the agenda of the winter session that began on Nov. 22. However, its status remained unchanged.
January 2013	The Cabinet approved a version of the bill that left out religious and charitable institutions aided by the government – a month before the Budget session that began on February 21.
August 2013	The bill was expected to be discussed during the monsoon session of the parliament which began on Aug. 5 but it retained its pending status at the end of the sitting.
December 5, 2013	With the winter session of the Parliament beginning, passing of the bill was top priority for the lawmakers as it threatened to become a major electoral issue if it remained pending.
December 17, 2013	Amendments to the Lokpal bill were passed by the Rajya Sabha from where the legislation was returned to the lower house for ratification.
13th December 2011-13	The government put the Lokpal Bill in the Rajya Sabha on 13 December 2013 and was adjourned till 16 December 2013 in want of debate. The Bill (The Lokpal and Lokayuktas Act, 2013) was passed in the Rajya Sabha on 17th December, 2013 after making certain amendments to the earlier Bill and in the Lok Sabha on 18th December, 2013.
2014	The Lokpal and Lokayuktas Act, 2013 received the assent of the President on the 1st January, 2014.

The table has shown that initially the concept was debated during 1960 and late lot of efforts were made to pass the lokpal bill but it was in year of 2013, almost after 50 years 'The Lokpal and Lokayuktas Act, 2013'was finally passed.

2.8 Lokpal Bill and the Prime Minister[77]

Since the idea of the institution like ombudsman was discussed in India, there have been issues that whether the office of the Prime Minister of India, should be brought down under the purview of the Lokpal. It was urged in to the report of the National Commission to Review the working of the Constitution that the Prime Minister should be kept out of the Purview of the Lokpal.[78] So what is the principle behind such immunity being given? The questions remain unanswered. Why the Prime Minister should not be under the purview of the Lokpal? Will the Investigation against the Prime Minister amount to disrespect to the office of the PM? Will Prime Minister being kept under the purview of the Lokpal amount to destabilisation of India? Under the Indian Constitution there is no provision to give immunity to the Prime minister, Chief Ministers or Ministers. Under Article 361, immunity from the criminal proceedings is conferred on the President and the Governor only "during his term of office."[79]

2.8.1 The Prime Minister v. the President Immunity

The Constitution of India did not provide for any immunity to PM, [80] whereas President enjoys it during the term of office. Article 361(2)[81] provided that no criminal proceedings whatsoever shall be instituted or continued against the President or the Governor of a State in any court during his term of office. There is a provision that the conduct of President may be brought under review by any court, tribunal or body appointed or designated by either House of Parliament for investigation of a charge under Article 61 of the Constitution of India (which provided for impeachment of President). Thus if Parliament wanted, it can designate a tribunal to question the actions of the President during his tenure. When the Constitution gave the authority to question the action of President by any designated tribunal, why not the actions of Prime Minister are brought under probe by Lokpal? The line is clearly drawn. Constitutional heads who do not directly exercise executive powers are given immunity as heads of state. Active Politicians such as Ministers, who cannot remain aloof from the hurly-burly of electoral and party politics, ethical or unethical, honest or corrupt, are not given any immunity. They are subject to penal laws and criminal liability. The Constitution clearly denies immunity to the Prime Minister.The council of Ministers shall be collectively responsible to the house of the people.[82] The Supreme Court of India in the case of *State of Karnataka* v. *Union of India*[83] held that the object of the collective responsibility is to make the whole body of the persons holding ministerial office collectively or vicariously responsible for such acts of the others as referable to their collective violation so that even if an individual may not be personally responsible for it, still he shall be deemed to share the responsibility with those who may have actually committed wrongs.

2.8.2 Proposed Immunity to Prime Minister during Internal Emergency

During the Period of the Internal Emergency (1975-77), the then Prime Minister of India Mrs Indira Gandhi exercised dictatorial powers. She detained without trial prominent opposition leaders and was supported by a captive and rump Parliament. The Constitutional 44th Amendment Bill was moved in, and passed by, Rajya Sabha in 1975 and later it was to go before the Lok Sabha. The Bill was blacked out from the media and hence very few people knew about it. It never became law because it was not moved in the Lok Sabha. The Bill sought to amend Article 361 to give life-time immunity from criminal proceedings for acts done during and even prior to assuming office, of the President, the Governor and additionally the Prime Minister did not materialise.

2.8.3 Foreign Jurisdictions[84]

In Japan, Prime Minister Kakuei Tanaka (July 1972 – December 1974) was found guilty of bribery and sentenced.[85] In Israel Prime Minister Ehud Olmert was indicted in corruption scandals in August 2009. In Italy Prime Minister Silvio Berlusconi enacted, through legislature, a law by which he shielded himself from prosecution. The Italian Constitutional Court invalidated crucial parts of the Law, which may result in his trial being revived.[86] What is the ground reality ? First, the CBI, is under the Department of Personnel and Training, which is controlled by the Prime Minister Office (PMO).[87] Secondly, the carrer prospects of CBI officers and other personnel are dependent on the political executive, and all officers are subject to transfer except the director.[88] Further in the case of Vineet Narain v. Union of India [89] the supreme court invalidated an administrative directive which was legislatively revived. Consequently, under Section 6A of the Delhi Special Police Establishment Act, the CBI is disabled from starting an inquiry or investigation against Joint Secretary or higher level bureaucrats without the Central government's prior approval. It is imperative that the CBI's anti-corruption wing be brought under the Lokpal and not under the PMO.it was argued that bringing the Prime Minister under the Lokpal's scrutiny would mean a parallel government being put in place.[90] This objection does not sustain. Do the Supreme Court and the higher judiciary constitute a parallel government? Is the CAG a parallel government? Is the CEC a parallel government? Is the CBI a parallel government?[91] So The Lokpal should be under the Constitution and subject to judicial review, and it is imperative that the anti-corruption wing of the CBI be brought under the Lokpal and the office of the Prime Minister Also.[92]

References

1. Donald C Rowat, *'Recent Development in Ombudsmanship. A review of Articles – Canadian Public Administration,* Vol.10. March 1967.'
2. Bernard Frank, "The Ombudsman Revisited", *International Bar Journal,* 55, 1975.

3. *Ibid.*
4. *Ibid.*
5. U.C. Agarwal, "Role of Lokpal in fostering ethical governance and society" Vol LIX, No.*3 Indian Journal of Public Administration* 432 (2013).
6. D.R. Saxena, *Ombudsman(Lokpal): redress of citizens in India,* 70 (Deep and Deep, New Delhi, 198*).*
7. M. P. Jain, *Lokpal: Ombudsman in India* 41 *(*Academic Books Limited, New Delhi, 1st edn., 1970).
8. Walter Gellhorn, *Ombudsmen and Others* 5 (Harvard University Press, Cambridge, 1967)
9. M. P. Jain, *Lokpal: Ombudsman in India* 45 *(*Academic Books Limited, New Delhi, 1st edn., 1970).
10. Girdhar B. Sharma, *Implementation of Ombudsman plan in India* 7 (Ashish Publishing House, New Delhi, 1st edn., 1981).
11. *Ibid.*
12. *Ibid.*
13. Chandra Shekhar Joshi, "Need of Lokpal as Legal Instrument for Prevention of Corruption in India" Vol 48- No.2 *Civil and Military Law Journal* 93 (2012).
14. *Ibid.*
15. *Id.*
16. *Id.*
17. *Id.*
18. *Id.*
19. Girdhar B. Sharma, *Implementation of Ombudsman plan in India* 24 (Ashish Publishing House, New Delhi, 1st edn., 1981).
20. *Ibid.*
21. *Ibid.*
22. *Ibid.*
23. M. P. Jain, *Lokpal Ombudsman in India* 1 (Academic Books limited, New Delhi, 1st edn., 1970).
24. *Ibid.*
25. *Ibid.*
26. Government of Rajasthan, *Report of the Administrative Reforms Committee* (Ministry of Law and Justice, 1963).
27. Government of India, Administrative Reform Commission, Interim Report: *on the Problem of Redress of Citizen's Grievances* (Ministry of Law and Justice, 1966).

28. *Ibid.*
29. *Ibid.*
30. Girdhar B. Sharma, *Implementation of Ombudsman plan in India* 26 (Ashish Publishing House, New Delhi, 1st edn., 198).
31. M. P. Jain, *Lokpal Ombudsman in India* 118 (Academic Books limited, New Delhi, 1st edn., 1970).
32. *Ibid.*
33. *Ibid.*
34. *Ibid.*
35. M. P. Jain, *Lokpal Ombudsman in India* 119 (Academic Books limited, New Delhi, 1st edn., 1970).
36. *Ibid.*
37. *Ibid.*
38. *Ibid.*
39. *Ibid.*
40. *Ibid.*
41. Government of India, Administrative Reform Commission, Interim Report: *on the Problem of Redress of Citizen's Grievances* (Ministry of Law and Justice, 1966).
42. *Ibid.*
43. *Ibid.*
44. *Ibid.*
45. *Ibid.*
46. M. P. Jain, *Lokpal Ombudsman in India* 129 (Academic Books limited, New Delhi, 1st edn., 1970).
47. *Ibid.*
48. M. P. Jain, *Lokpal Ombudsman in India* 129(Academic Books limited, New Delhi, 1st edn., 1970).
49. *Ibid.*
50. *Ibid.*
51. *Ibid.*
52. *Ibid.*
53. Issues related to the Lokpal Bill, national commission to review the working of the Constitution(2002), India, *available* at : *http://www.prsindia.org/administrator/uploads/general/1302082895_Issue%20Brief%20on%20Lok%20Pal%20Bil.pdf (Visited* on February 5, 2014).

54. Issues related to the Lokpal Bill, Second Administrative Reform commission(2007), India, available at *http://www.prsindia.org/administrator/uploads/general/1302082895_Issue%20Brief%20on%20Lok%20Pal%20Bil.pdf(Visited* on February 6, 2014).
55. *Ibid.*
56. *Ibid.*
57. *Ibid.*
58. *Ibid.*
59. *Ibid.*
60. *Ibid.*
61. *Ibid.*
62. *Ibid.*
63. *Ibid.*
64. *Ibid.*
65. *Ibid.*
66. *Ibid.*
67. *Ibid.*
68. *Ibid.*
69. *Ibid.*
70. Government of India, Administrative Reform Commission, Interim Report: *on the Problem of Redress of Citizen's Grievances* (Ministry of Law and Justice, 1966).
71. *Ibid.*
72. *Ibid.*
73. "Executive and Public administration, " Chapter 6 of the National Commission to Review the working of the Constitution (Chairperson: Still M.N.Venkatachaliah), March 31, 2002.
74. National Common Minimum Programme of the Government of India, India, available at: *http://pib.nic.in/archieve/others/2005/hs01mar2k5.pdf (visited* on February 27, 2014).
75. Lokpal and Lokayukta Act, 2013.
76. A Brief time line of the Lokpal Bill, India, *available at: http://www.prsindia.org/administrator/uploads/general/1302860449_Lok%20Pal%20Bill%20Timeline.pdf(Visited* on March 02, 2013*),* see also Timeline: The Lokpal's long walk to Law, India, *available at* : *http://blogs.wsj.com/indiarealtime/2013/12/18/timeline-the-lokpals-long-walk-to-law/(Visited* on March 03, 2013).

77. Lokpal and the Prime Minister, India, ***available at***: ***http://www.thehindu.com/opinion/lead/lokpal-bill-and-the-prime-minister/article2148073.ece***(*Visited* on March 26, 2014).
78. *Ibid.*
79. Article 361 of the Constitution of India.
80. *http://indiacurrentaffairs.org/excluding-pm-from-lokpal-unconstitutional-prof-madabhushi-sridhar/*(*Visited* on March 27, 2014
81. Article 361(2) of the Constitution of India.
82. Article 75(3) of the Constitution of India.
83. *State of Karnataka* v. *Union of India*, AIR 1978 SC 68.
84. Lokpal and the Prime Minister, India, available at: ***http://www.thehindu.com/opinion/lead/lokpal-bill-and-the-prime-minister/article2148073.ece***(*Visited* on March 26, 2014).
85. *Ibid.*
86. *Ibid.*
87. Lokpal and the Prime Minister, India, ***available at***: ***http://www.thehindu.com/opinion/lead/lokpal-bill-and-the-prime-minister/article2148073.ece***(*Visited* on March 26, 2014).
88. *Ibid.*
89. *Vineet Narain and Others* v. *Union of India*(1996)2 SCC 158.
90. Lokpal and the Prime Minister, India, ***available at***: ***http://www.thehindu.com/opinion/lead/lokpal-bill-and-the-prime-minister/article2148073.ece***(*Visited* on March 26, 2014).
91. *Ibid.*
92. *Ibid.*

Chapter – 3

Ombudsman-Sweden and United Kingdom *vis-a-vis* India

> *The pressure for rapid development implies that individual rights and the fine points of fair legal procedures are more likely to be disregarded in the interests of speed, efficiency and the broader public interest. Also the bureaucrats in many former colonies have inherited from their colonial masters an attitude of superiority, rather than service, an insolence of office which often leads to arbitrariness.*[1]

To understand the institution of Ombudsman, It would be better to understand it globally. The Ombudsman institution has gained widespread acceptance in many countries, this symbolises the fact that human problems are the same throughout the world and their solutions are essentially similar.[2] Governments enjoy a monopoly of power in dictating the quality of life for their citizens.[3]

Public sector agencies provide vital services such as security, communications, social welfare and public utilities, electricity water, health, transport and education.[4] The provision of such services is regulated by policies formulated by the government departments.[5] In India the seventh schedule of the Constitution of India makes the elaborate provision in this regard.[6] While these policies are being formulated government agencies has a vital say including legislative drafting.[7] In the process of implementing, government policy affecting these services, those entrusted with authority exercise very wide discretionary powers, this renders the citizen vulnerable to the decisions of those public officials.[8]

India having a welfare Consitution has additional responsibility. Moreover the democratic process is three tier which mandates the policymakers to be more citizen friendly. Therefore huge moner is utilized in welfare activities for example MNREGA Act 2005[9], NRHM[10] etc. where big government money is involved, corrupt practices, arbitrariness, misuse of authority, discrimination etc. are not far behind.

To avoid arbitrariness, abuse of power or office, discriminatory practices, offensive conduct, illegal and erroneous practices, social injustices and inefficiency, the institution of an ombudsman, was developed with a view of government itself should provide an independent office to monitor the implementation of policy and the provision of services to ensure administrative justice and fair treatment of all the people.[11]

The Ombudsman institution has been appreciated in countries where it operates as an agent of the people and protector of their rights against government bureaucratic injustices.[12] The other side of the coin is that the same ombudsman institution can be used by the government as a cleansing tool to tick abuse of power and ensure that the rule of law is observed by the government agencies, that such observance of rule of law applies from the highest ranks to the ranks below.[13] Where the ombudsman institution operates effectively, it gives a human face to government and guarantees acceptance of government by the people.[14] In such systems, power and privileged is not used to suppress the powerless and the least privileged, rather, the ombudsman institution is used as a medium of transferring power to the people to whom it belongs.[15]

In India Supreme Court of India and High Courts are working very effectively and came down heavily to tackle corruption cases and also issued guidelines in this regard[16] but a Lokpal is a necessity because Courts are not meant for this.

At the 1991 Harare Sommit of Commonwealth Heads of Government, a consensus communiqué was released by the delegates to the effect that fundamental political values of the Commonwealth countries would be democracy, democratic process and the establishment of institutions which reflect the rule of law, and a just and honest government.[17]

The quest for social justice and fair treatment of all people cannot, therefore be over emphasised. How else can government accountability and transparency be achieved? The institution of the ombudsman answers the question.[18] Looking at the success of the institution of Ombudsman abroad, and for addressing the issue of corruption, 'The Lokpal and Lokayuktas Act, 2013' was passed in India. But the question still stands, about the success of the redressal mechanism, so the author has undertaken comparative study of the Ombudsman in Sweden and Britain with instituion of Lokpal in India since the institution firstly emerged in Sweden, he undertook to highlight it in Sweden.

3.1 Sweden

Professor Gellhorn has rightly observed :

> Much of the Swedish Constitution has been forgotten. Its delineation of royal powers and parliamentary structure has little relevance to today realities. But the office it created that of 'Justitie Ombudsman' has lived and grown. It has inspired similar establishment in Finland, Denmark, Norway, New Zealand and in many other countries and has added the word 'Ombudsman' to the international vocabulary.[19]

The institution of the ombudsman in Sweden has gained widespread attention in the democratic world as a device for controlling bureaucracy.[20] The Swedish Ombudsmen are at once the longest established and the most powerful of all

Ombudsmen.[21] The word "ombudsman" is quite common in Swedish. It means representative or attorney.[22] In Sweden several hundred people are called ombudsman. Trade Unions have ombudsman, and so do banks and insurance companies.[23]

The parliamentary ombudsman, who are officers of the Riksdag (The Swedish Parliament).[24] They supervise state and municipal authorities to ensure that the authorities properly fulfil their obligations.[25] Their official title is justitieom-budsman (ombudsman for justice) or JO as they are commonly known.[26]

In previous chapter historical development of Lokpal is discussed. It is also desirable to know the background in Sweden because it will help to understand various things like need of the institution and reasons etc.

3.1.1 Historical Background

Although the office of the *justitieombudsman* was created in 1809, it had an older counterpart.[27] When King Charles XII of Sweden was defeated in the battle of Poltava in Russia (1709), he had to flee to Turkey where he stayed for many years.[28] To Stop the unrest and disorder which was rife in Sweden, the King issued an order in 1713 that an office should be created in Sweden to be headed by the king's highest ombudsman.[29] This office later known as chancellor of justice (justitiekansler).[30] From 1766 to 1772, the Riksdag, which had taken over practically all power from the King exercised the right to appoint the chancellor of justice.[31]

In 1809, King Gustav IV Adolf, who had reigned as an absolute despot, was dethroned. The Riksdag was convened for the first time in many years, and it decided to adopt a new Constitution based on the principle of a balance of power between king and Riksdag.[32] The Constitution contained provisions for appointment by the king of a chancellor of justice and for the election by the Riksdag of a *justitieombudsman.*[33]

The First ombudsman (Baron L.A. Mannerheim) was elected in 1810. In 1915, the Riksdag found it necessary to separate the function of supervising the military authorities from the general supervisory functions of the *justitieombudsman* created a separate office for the control of the armed forces – *the militieombudsman* (military commissioner).

In 1968, the two offices of the *justitieombudsman* and the *militieombudsman* were amalgamated. Since 1968, the workload of the ombudsman has increased heavily. It became necessary to reorganise the office. Further some, an amendment to the Penal Code, Effective January 1, 1976, made it essential to issue new rules for the Ombudsman's supervision. In 1975, the Riksdag adopted a new Instruction to the Parliamentary Ombudsman containing new rules for the organisation of their office as well as for their duties and powers.

3.1.2 Table No. 3 Development of the Institution of the Ombudsman in Sweden.

Year	*Development of the Institution of the Ombudsman*
1713	The King Charles XII of Sweden issued an order in 1713 that an office should be created in Sweden to be headed by the king's highest ombudsman.
1766-1772	The Riksdag, which had taken over practically all power from the King exercised the right to appoint the chancellor of justice.
1810	The First ombudsman (Baron L.A. Mannerheim) was elected.
1915	The Riksdag found it necessary to separate the function of supervising the military authorities from the general supervisory functions of the *justitieombudsman* created a separate office for the control of the armed forces – *the militieombudsman* (military commissioner).
1951	A Military Ombudsman was appointed in Sweden.
1968	The two offices of the *justitieombudsman* and the *militieombudsman* were amalgamated.

1972	Parliament (The Riksdag) appointed a Committee to look in to the Problem.
1975	The Parliament recommended a new form of organisation and a number of amendments to the statutes regulating the Ombudsmen's work.
1976	The Riksdag adopted a new Instruction to the Parliamentary Ombudsman containing new rules for the organisation of their office as well as for their duties and powers. The recommendations were approved by Parliament in November 1975 and the new system came in to effect in the spring of 1976.

In Sweden initially the concept of ombudsman started with the order of the The King Charles XII of Sweden during eighteenth century and later during the nineteenth century the first ombudsman was appointed. So it is very important to know that what is the procedure of appointment in Sweden.

3.1.2 Method of Appointment of Ombudsman

In Sweden, the Ombudsman[34] is elected by a special committee of 48 persons chosen for the purpose by Parliament from amongst its members—24 from each of the two Houses of Parliament.[35] Voting is by ballot. He is elected for a period of four years but he may be re-elected for further terms.[36] His salary equals that of Supreme Court Judge.[37] He is responsible to Parliament to which he submits an annual report containing a general account of his activities and a detailed account of the more important cases dealt with by him during the year.[38] Every year a parliamentary committee reviews the working of the Ombudsman and it may recommend to Parliament his dismissal if it feels that he does not deserve the confidence of Parliament and should be relieved of his office before the expiry of his term.[39]

Parliament can not issue any instructions to the Ombudsman as to which case he should investigate ; he is free from any influence while investigating a particular case.[40] The Swedish Constitution declares about the qualification for Ombudsman should be person of "Known legal ability and outstanding integrity."[41] So the author undertakes the work of highlighting the powers of Ombudsman in Sweden.

3.1.3 The Ombudsman's Powers

In Sweden The Ombudsmen's supervision covers all state and municipal agencies and bodies as well as their personnel.[42] The Swedish Ombudsman is by no means super administrator.[43] He is not empowered to overturn every error and to produce correct answers to all the difficult questions which the government confronts.[44]

As representative of the Parliament and pursuant to its instruction he should 'supervise the observance of the laws and status as they may be applied "by the court and by public officials and employees".[45] Supervision, as the Parliament instructions make clear, does not include control over what judges and administrators do.[46] He does not give orders. He cannot reverse a decision. But certainly he can prosecute an official he believes to be a guilty of crime of breach of duty.[47] Thus the powers JO (Justitie Ombudsman) as defined in the Constitution are:[48]

i. To supervise how judges, government officials and other civil servants observe the laws;[49] and
ii. To prosecute those who have acted illegally or have neglected their duties.[50]

3.1.3.1 As Supervisor

To perform his supervisory duties the JO has access to all documents even secret ones, and the right to be present at all documents at which judges or administrative officials make their rulings.[51] The JO is thereby assured a complete view of all legal and administrative activities.

3.1.3.2 As a Prosecutor

The JO has the right to ask for assistance of any officials for the purpose making necessary investigations and all prosecuting attorneys must perform any prosecution the JO may desire.[52] It is important to compare India here because 'The Lokpal and Lokayuktas Act, 2013' does have provision to prosecute.

3.1.5 Ombudsman's Jurisdiction

In Sweden his jurisdiction embraces all National and Municipal Officials.

3.1.5.1 Ministers

Members of Government however are exempt from his control.[53] Parliament may order the prosecution of a minister before a special court. Ombudsman acts as Prosecutor in cases of this kind.[54] In Sweden so far as no opinion has been expressed that the Ombudsman's authority should be extended to the ministers as well.

3.1.5.2 Military

Earlier all military Commanders and officers of the lower rank were under the supervision of JO. Since 1915, the Constitution has provided a separate Ombudsman for Military affairs[55] with the same qualifications and chosen in the same manner as the Ombudsman for the Civil Affairs. Since 1968, JO's and MO's offices have been amalgamated.[56]

3.1.5.3 Judges

In case of serious misdemeanour only Ombudsman can take action against the member of supreme court of Justice and members of Supreme administrative court and not otherwise.[57] Swedish judges are not influenced in their decisions by the power of the Ombudsman to survey the activities of the court.[58]

3.1.5.4 Local Government

Since 1957, all the Municipal Boards and officials expecting elected members or the Municipal Councils are subject to the Ombudsman's attention.[59]

3.1.6 Function and Procedure

3.1.6.1 Grounds For Supervision

Courts, Prosecutors, Police and Prisons Departments were under the control of Ombudsman. Improper behaviour of the officials and abuse of official position by them are the main grounds for causing intervention of the Ombudsman in the affairs of administration.

3.1.6.2 Nature and Sources of Ombudsman's work

As Parliament's watchman, he can and does proceed on his own motion when problems come to his attention through newspaper stories, personal conversation, suggestions by officials themselves, or his own periodic inspection of the courts and administrative agencies.[60] The range of subject matters are courts (excluding administrative courts), public Prosecutors, Police authorities, Child and youth welfare, school administration, tax authorities, church authorities etc.[61]

3.1.6.3 Complaints

Everyone –even citizens of other countries or people not living in Sweden- can complain to the Ombudsmen.[62] Complaints have to be presented in writing. When necessary, a member of the ombudsman's staff will help complainants to word their letters. No fee is charged. Anonymous complaints are not admissible. In 1963, the *Justitieombudsman* and the militieombudsman received 1, 300 complaints, in 1968, 2, 120 complaints, and 1979, 3, 145[63] under following Table No. 4 the data has been provided to show the out come of the complaints which were received by the office of the Ombudsman in Sweden.

3.1.6.4 Table No. 4[64]

Typical outcomes of complaints to the Ombudsman office in Sweden

Outcome	*Percentage*
Dismissed as being outside jurisdiction or of obscure meaning	3.75
Dismissed for other reasons without investigation	38.00
Referred to other agencies	2.00
No criticism after investigation	44.00
Admonition, recommendations, and so forth	12.00
Prosecutions or disciplinary proceedings	0.20
Proposals to the government	0.05

In the first one hundred years of the office's existence, the ombudsman received about seventy complaints a year.[65] On an average, only 12 per cent of all cases give rise to some kind of action on the part of the Ombudsman.[66] No less than 38 per cent are dismissed without full investigation, although formally they do not fall outside the ombudsman's jurisdiction.[67] The continually growing number of complaints has made it necessary for the ombudsman to dismiss immediately complaints that seem to be minor importance.[68] As shown, about 38 per cent of all complaints are thus dismissed without investigation.[69]

3.1.6.5 Investigation and Methods of Supervision Initiated by The Ombudsman[70]

Many Investigations are started on the ombudsman's own initiative.[71] The Majority of these are based on observations made during inspections, but in a number of cases newspaper reports of the activities have given the ombudsman cause to open an investigation.[72] So have programmes on television. Furthermore, when investigating a complaint, the ombudsman sometimes discovers unsatisfactory conditions or errors committed are not covered by the complaint.[73] They will then act on their own initiative and open a new investigation.[74] Sometimes an anonymous letter, which is not admissible as a complaint, will cause an ombudsman to intervene formally on his own initiative.[75]

3.1.6.6 Ombudsman's Method of Supervision

The Methods used in cases initiated by the ombudsman are more less the same as those used in the complaint cases. As an Ombudsman does not open an investigation without good reason, it is understandable that a higher percentage of these cases result in some kind of action than of the complaint cases. Ever since the office was set up in 1810, the ombudsman has from time made inspections of the courts, prisons, and administrative agencies all over the country.[76] The Ombudsman used to spend 30 working days a year each on inspections, excluding those by staff members.[77] The figure has been increased to seventy four days, despite efforts to reduce routine inspections.

During the inspections, much time is spent in perusing files and documents. Interviews are held with the head of the board, office, or establishment concerned.[78] In addition, some of the officials will normally be interviewed.[79] When a prison, mental hospital is inspected the inmates are given the opportunity of talking to the ombudsman and expressing their grievances. An Inspection may reveal errors in individual's cases which subsequently can be rectified.[80] He initiated investigations without motivated by the complaint.[81] He freely undertakes these investigations on the basis of the reports of the courts or administrative officials that appears in the newspaper.[82]

It is worth mentioning here that the intervention by Ombudsman is not limited to deal with the mistakes and acts of negligence that have been committed, but he also follows up to see if the injured parties have been compensated.[83] The Ombudsman may also appeal to the government for compensation to a complainant and such an appeal is almost successful.[84] In cases of unjust punishments, JO has tried to help the convicted person either to get a new trial or appeal to the Government for Clemency.[85]

3.1.6.7 Right to appeal against the Ombudsman's Decision

There is no express provision of law in Sweden to appeal, against the decision of Ombudsman. Presently Ombudsman's decision can be reviewed, re-opened or appealed in the following circumstances:[86]

i. The Ombudsman himself can review and reopen the case in case of the further evidence brought for his attention.[87]
ii. He feels that he has overlooked some provision of law, may change his opinion.[88]
iii. An official who is dissatisfied with the admonition may ask the Ombudsman to prosecute him and so let the Court decide whether he has committed a fault.[89]

3.1.7 Report And Action

3.1.7.1 Parliament's Control

His parliamentary relationship is with one of the standing committees, the 'First Law Committee' which happens to be under the chairmanship of an opposition member. The annual report submitted by the Ombudsman to the Parliament is reviewed by the Committee.[90] When reporting to the Parliament, the committee may criticise the ombudsman's decision.[91] The Committee may even propose that Parliament should dismiss the Ombudsman before his term of office is over.[92] In spite of the fact that the Committee has wide powers to control the activities of Ombudsman, but in reality he is entirely independent of the Government.[93]

3.1.7.2 Annual Report

The Ombudsman's one of the duties is to present an annual report to the Parliament.[94] It includes the work performed by him, investigations he has made during the past year. According to Mr Alfred Bexelius "This report is probably the JO's most important means of influencing the application of the laws in Sweden."[95]

3.1.8 Position of Courts & Judges

Courts[96] are not hierarchically organised. Each Judge applies the law as he sees it. He alone is responsible for the correctness of judgement delivered by him. Sweden's ordinary courts of law possess very little powers. They cannot command an official to do an act nor restrain its being done. They cannot issue declaratory orders too. In short, they have no effective and significant role to play. They can only punish an administrator for violating the law.

In a technical sense the Ombudsman fits into this system of 'Individual responsibility' instead of 'institutional responsibility'. He simply acts as a prosecutor who can proceed against official wrong doers before the tribunal authorised[97] to mete out the punishment.[98]

1.2 The British Ombudsman

In the late fifties and the beginning of sixties in the U.K., in was felt that there was a need for an adequate machinery for the redress of citizen's grievances against administration.[99] The emerging belief that the Minister's own accountability to Parliament was no longer sufficient to protect the victim of the Departmental error and maladministration, led to the establishment of the office of Parliamentary Commissioner in 1967.[100] The Parliamentary commissioner for Administration in the United Kingdom began to investigate complaints on 1 April 1967.[101]

3.2.1 Appointment

The Parliamentary commissioner for Administration is to be appointed by Her Majesty.[102] He holds his office during good behaviour.[103] He may be removed form office earlier by Her

Majesty in consequence of addresses from both houses of Parliament.[104] His salary, pension and other benefits payable under the Act are chagred on the consilidated Fund.[105] The Commissioner may delegate his function to any of his officers. He makes a general report to Parliament every year and special reports from time to time as he thinks fit particularly when he thinks that the injustice caused to an aggrieved person has not been, or will not be remedied.[106]

3.2.2 Jurisdiction

His area of jurisdiction is closely defined by the Act itself.[107] The bodies to be subject to investigation by the commissioner in matters within his scope are listed in the statute.[108]

Following are the conditions precedent for the purpose of exercising jurisdiction, or conducting investigation of complaints, by the commissioner:

i. Firstly: A written complaint must be made to a Member of the House of Commons by a member of public, who claims to have sustained injustice, in consequence of maladministration;[109] and
ii. Secondly: Then the said complaint should be reffered to the Commissioner with the consent of the person who made it by a Member of the house with a request to conduct an investigation thereon;[110]
iii. Important matters which are not subject to the investigation by the commissioner are as follows;[111]
iv. Action taken in matters certified by a Secretary of the state or other Ministers of the crown to affect relations or dealing between the U.K. government and any other government, or international organisation.[112]
v. Action taken outside the U.K by an officer representing or acting under;
vi. the authority of the Crown.[113]

vii. The Administration of colonial or independent territories outside the U.K.

viii. Action taken by the Secratary of State under the Extradition Act, 1870 or the Fugitive Offenders Act, 1881.[114]

ix. Any exercise of the prerogative of mercy.[115]

x. Matters relating to contractual or other commercial transactions on the part of Central Government.[116]

3.2.3 Function and Powers

A significant feature of the functioning of the Ombudsman in England is that he does not receive complaints directly from the people.[117] Complaints to him are routed through members of the House of Commons. The Ombudsman, therefore, acts only at the instance of a member of the House of Commons which is the elected representative body in Parliament.[118] The person complaining of any personal injury suffered by him complains writing to a member of the House of the Commons and it is for him to decide whether the complaint is appropriate for reference to the Ombudsman.[119] In case the person has died or is unable to act for himself, the complaint may be made by his personal representative or a member of his family or any other individual suitable to represent him.[120] Visitors from abroad are included if the complaint relates to something which happens while they are lawfully present in the United Kingdom.[121]

The British Ombudsman is required to make his invesigation in private, removed from the gaze of publicity, and is free to adopt such procedure as he may consider appropriate in the circumstances of the case.[122]

The Commissioner has the same powers as a court in respect of the attendance and examination of witness and production of documents.[123] If a person obstructs the Ombudsman without lawful excuse in the performance of his fuctions, or if he is guilty of an act or ommission in relation to an investigation by him which would amount to contempt of court had the proceedings been before the court, the ombudsman may certify the offence to the court.[124] Before conducting the investigation, the Ombudsman has to give the principal officer of the department of the authority concerned an opportunity to comment on any of the allegations made in the complaint.[125]

In any case, where the Ombudsman conducts an investigation, he has also to send a report of the results of the investigation to the department or authority concerned.[126] If after investigation, it appears to the ombudsman that injustice has been caused to the person aggrieved in consequence of maladministration and that the injustice has not been remedied, he may if he thinks fit, lay before each House of Parliament a special report upon the case.[127] Each year the ombudsman is to lay before each house of Parliament a general report on the performance of his functions and may from time to time may before each house of Parliament such other reports with respect to these functions as he thinks fit.[128]

3.2.4 Sanctions

In England, the Ombudsman has no power to initiate any prosecutions or to issue reminders to the civil servants found to be at fault.[129] If after consideration of a complaint, he finds nothing wrong, he informs accordingly the member of Parliament who approached him. If he finds that there is justifiable cause for complaint and the department responds to his invitation to put it right, he will inform the member accordingly.[130] It is for the Parliament to decide, with the help of the committee when established, to consider what action should be taken on the report, special or annual.[131] The Ombudsman in his annual report may comment on defects in the system which come to his notice as a result of investigating individual complaints.[132]

3.3 Lokpal in India Under 'The Lokpal and Lokayuktas Act, 2013'

3.3.1 Establishment of Lokpal[133]

According to section 3(2) of 'The Lokpal and Lokayuktas Act, 2013' The Lokpal shall consist of—

(a) a Chairperson, who is or has been a Chief Justice of India or is or has been a Judge of the Supreme Court or an eminent person who fufills the eligibility specified in clause (b) of sub-section (3); and

(b) such number of Members and not exceeding eight out of whom fifty percent shall be Judicial Members.

3.3.2 Appointment of Chairperson and Members of Lokpal

It is provided under section 4[134] the Chairperson and other Members of the Lokpal shall be appointed obtaining the recommendations of a Selection Committee consisting of the Prime Minister, the Speaker of the House of the People, the leader of the Oppositionin the House of the People, the Chief Justice of India or a Judge of the Supreme Court nominated by him, one eminent jurist as recommended by the Chairperson and members referred in clauses (a) to (d), to be nominated by the President. For the purpose of holding the Chairperson and other Members of the Lokpal and for preparing a panel of persons to be considered for appointment, the Selection Committee may constitute a Search Committee consisting of such persons having special knowledge and expertise in the matters relating to anti-corruption policy, public administration, vigilance, policy making, finance including insurance and banking, law and management or in any other matter which in the opinion of the Selection Committtee may be useful for making the selection of a Chairperson and Members of the Lokpal. It further provides that the Selection Committee shall regulate its own procedure in a transparent manner for selecting the Chairperson and Members of the Lokpal.

3.3.3 Powers of Lokpal

Powers of the Lokpal has been given under sections 25 to 34 of 'The Lokpal and Lokayuktas Act, 2013. The Lokpal shall have the powers of superindence over, and to give direction, to the Delhi Special police Establishment in respect of the matters referred by the Lokpal for preliminary inquiry or investigation to the Delhi Special Police Establishment under the Lokpal Act.[135] Lokpal shall have the all the powers of the civil courts in certain cases.[136] Lokpal may delegate powers.[137]

As per Section 12 of 'The Lokpal and Lokayuktas Act, 2013

(1) The Lokpal shall, by notification, *constitute a Prosecution Wing headed by the Director of Prosecution for the purpose of prosecution of public servants* in relation to any complaint by the Lokpal under this Act:

Provided that till such time the *Prosecution Wing* is constituted by the Lokpal, the Central Government shall make available such number of officers and other staff from its Ministries or Departments, as may be required by the Lokpal, for conducting prosecution under this Act.

(2) The *Director of Prosecution shall*, after having been so directed by the Lokpal, file a case in accordance with the findings of investigation report, before the Special Court and take all necessary steps in respect of the prosecution of public servants in relation to any offence punishable under the Prevention of Corruption Act, 1988.

(3) The case under sub-section (*2*), shall be deemed to be a report, filed on completion of investigation, referred to in section 173 of the Code of Criminal Procedure, 1973.

Now the author wants to address the jurisdictional power of the Ombudsman in Sweden and India. [Emphasis added]

3.3.4 Jurisdiction of Lokpal

Section 14 of the Lokpal Act,[138] discusses about the jurisdiction of the Lokpal in respect of inquiry. The jurisdiction of Lokpal includes Prime Minister, Ministers, members of Parliament, Group A, B, C and D officers and officials of Central Government. Under section 2(o) 'public servant' means a person reffered to in clauses (a) to (h) of sub-section (1) of section 14 of 'The Lokpal and Lokayuktas Act, 2013' but does not include a public servant in respect of whom the jurisdiction is exercisable by any court or other authority under the Army Act, 1950, the Air Force Act, 1957 and the Coast Guard Act, 1978. So Military is excluded from the purview of the Lokpal Act. 'Public servant' means a person reffered to in clauses (a) to (h) of sub-section (1) of the 'The Lokpal and Lokayuktas Act, 2013' which does not include the Judges.

3.3.5 Complaint

Under 'The Lokpal and Lokayuktas Act, 2013', "complaint" means, a complaint made in such form as may be prescribed, alleging that a public servant has committed an offence punishable under the Prevention of Corruption Act, 1988 (49 of 1988).[139] It is further provided in the Act that The Lokpal on receipt of a complaint, if it decides to proceed further and may order preliminary inquiry and investigation.[140] So under 'The Lokpal and Lokayuktas Act, 2013', it has not been specifically mentioned that 'who can camplaint?' for understanding the redressal mechanism better follwing Table No. 5 has shown the comparative study of Sweden, United Kingdom and India.

3.3.6 *Table No. 5*

Comparative Study of the Ombudsman in Sweden, United Kingdom and India

Country	*Name of Institution*	*Appointment Process*	*Power*	*Jurisdiction*	*Position of Judges*
Sweden	Justitie Ombudsman	He is elected by a special committee of 48 persons chosen for the purpose by Parliament from amongst its members-24 from each of two houses of Parliament.	As supervisor-To supervise how judges, govt officials and other civil servants observe the laws.As Prosecutor-The JO has right to take assistance of any offcials during investigation.	Ministers are exempted. For Military-separate Ombudsman Judges-in cases of serious misde-meanour. All Municipal Boards and Councils.	Courts not hierarchically organised. cannot issue declaratory orders too. Ordinary courts have little power.
United Kingdom	Parliamentary Commissioner	Appointed by Her Majesty.	Same as of courts.No power against civil servants.	Bodies covered are listed in the statute itself.	
India	Lokpal	The Chairperson and Members shall be appointed by the President on recommendation of a Selection Committee.It may constitute a Search Committee for the purpose of holding the Chairperson and Menbers of Lokpal and for preparing a panel of persons to be considered for appointment.	(i) As Supervisor-to give direction to the DSPE in respect of matters referred by the Lokpal for inquiry and investigation. (ii) As Courts- in certain cases. (iii) Power to utelise the services of officers of Central/State Govt. (iv) Power to delegate.	Prime Ministers, Ministers, Members of Parliament, Groups A, B, C and D officers and Officials of Central Government. Military and Judges are excluded.	Courts are hierarchically organised.Courts are very powerful and independent.

3.3.7 Comments

As shown above in the Table No 5 the Ombudsman of the three countries namely Sweden, United Kingdom and India have been discussed. The author has taken the countries of Sweden and United Kingdom reason being the former is the first country to have 'ombudsman' and where the institution of Ombudsman worked effectively. However, the reason for choosing the later one is of its been a Parliamentary country. By comparing the Ombudsman in Sweden and United Kingdom, it is found that ombudsman worked effectively in those countries where the Judicial system is not very strong. In India the Judicial System is very strong and it had been working effectively and had been able to win the confidence of the people in the largest democracy. He has apprehension about the working of the institution of Lokpal effectively in India which made the author to critically examine 'The Lokpal and Lokayutas Act, 2013.'

References

1. Donald C Rowat, *'Recent Development in Ombudsmanship. A review of Articles – Canadian Public Administration*, Vol.10. March 1967'
2. Madam Justice Florence N. Mumba, "The Ombudsman: The need for Protection and Control" in Norman Lewis, S.S. Singh et. al.(eds), *Ombudsman India and The World Community,* 33(1995).
3. *Ibid.*
4. *Ibid.*
5. *Ibid.*
6. Seventh Schedule Under Article 246 of the Constitution of India, provides for Three Lists, Union list, State List and Concurrent List, empowering the Union and the state to make laws on specific subjects.
7. *Ibid.*
8. *Ibid.*
9. Mahatma Gandhi National Rural Employment Gurantee Act, 2005, aims to aims to guarantee the 'right to work' and ensure livelihood security in rural areas by providing at least 100 days of guaranteed wage employment in a financial year to every household whose adult members volunteer to do unskilled manual work.

10. The National Rural Health Mission (NHRM) is an initiative undertaken by the Government of India to address the health needs of underserved rural areas.
11. *Ibid.*
12. Madam Justice Florence N. Mumba, "The Ombudsman: The need for Protection and Control" in Norman Lewis, S.S. Singh et.al. (eds), *Ombudsman India and The World Community,* 34 (1995).
13. *Ibid.*
14. *Ibid.*
15. *Ibid.*
16. *Vineet Narain* v. *Union of India* [1998, Cri LJ 1208, 1997(6) SCALE 16].
17. Madam Justice Florence N. Mumba, "The Ombudsman: The need for Protection and Control" in Norman Lewis, S.S. Singh et.al. (eds), *Ombudsman India and The World Community,* 35 (1995).
18. *Ibid.*
19. D. R. Saxena, *Ombudsman (Lokpal): redress of citizens in India, 33* (Deep and Deep, New Delhi, 1987).
20. Donald C. Rowat (ed.), *The Ombudsman* 7 (George Allen & Unwin Ltd., London, 1968).
21. Frank Stacey, *Ombudsman Compared'* 1 (Oxford, London, 1978).
22. Gerald E. Caiden, "International Handbook of the Ombudsman" 2 *Country Surveys*, 179 (1983).
23. *Ibid.*
24. *Ibid.*
25. *Ibid.*
26. *Ibid.*
27. Gerald E. Caiden, "International Handbook of the Ombudsman" 2 *Country Surveys*, 179 (1983).
28. *Ibid.*
29. *Ibid.*
30. *Ibid.*
31. *Ibid.*
32. *Ibid.*
33. *Ibid.*
34. He is officially designated as justitie Ombudsman. There is also an Ombudsman for Military affairs known as Militie Ombudsman.

35. M.P. Jain, *Lokpal: Ombudsman in India* 38 (Academic Books Limited, New Delhi, 1st edn., 1970).
36. Walter Gellhorn, *Ombudsmen and Others* 203 (Harvard University Press, Massachusetts, 1967).
37. *Ibid.*
38. M.P. Jain, *Lokpal : Ombudsman in India* 38 (Academic Books Limited, New Delhi, 1st edn., 1970)
39. *Ibid.*
40. *Ibid.*
41. Article 96 of the Constitution. See also : S. Jagerskiold, "The Swedish Constitution : A Survey" 5, *J.I.L.I.* (1963).
42. Gerald E. Caiden, "International Handbook of the Ombudsman" 2 *Country Surveys*, 180 (1983).
43. D. R. Saxena, *Ombudsman (Lokpal): redress of citizens in India,* 45 (Deep and Deep, New Delhi, 1987).
44. *Ibid.*
45. Article 96 of the Swedish Constitution.
46. D. R. Saxena, *Ombudsman(Lokpal): redress of citizens Grievances in India* 45 (Deep and Deep Publications, New Delhi, 1987).
47. Walter Gellhorn, Ombudsmen and Others 203 (Harvard University Press, Massachusetts, 1967).
48. D.R. Saxena, *Ombudsman (Lokpal): redress of citizens Grievances in India* 46 (Deep and Deep Publications, New Delhi, 1987).
49. *Ibid.*
50. *Ibid.*
51. *Ibid.*
52. *Ibid.*
53. In Denmark and Norway the ministers are under the supervision of Ombudsman.
54. Ministers can not give administrative officials binding orders. The officials are nonetheless completely independent. They have to follow the laws only.
55. Militie Ombudsman or MO.
56. D.R. Saxena, *Ombudsman(Lokpal): redress of citizens Grievances in India* 48 (Deep and Deep Publications, New Delhi, 1987).
57. *Ibid.*
58. *Ibid.*

59. *Ibid.*
60. Walter Gellhorn, *Ombudsmen and Others* 208 (Harvard University Press, Cambrigde, 1967).
61. D.R. Saxena, *Ombudsman (Lokpal): redress of citizens Grievances in India* 49 (Deep and Deep Publications, New Delhi, 1987).
62. Gerald E. Caiden, "International Handbook of the Ombudsman" 2 *Country Surveys*, 182 (1983).
63. Gerald E. Caiden, "International Handbook of the Ombudsman" 2 *Country Surveys*, 182 (1983).
64. Gerald E. Caiden, "International Handbook of the Ombudsman" 2 *Country Surveys*, 182 (1983).
65. *Ibid.*
66. *Ibid.*
67. *Ibid.*
68. *Ibid.*
69. *Ibid.*
70. Gerald E. Caiden, "International Handbook of the Ombudsman" 2 *Country Surveys*, 182 (1983).
71. Gerald E. Caiden, "International Handbook of the Ombudsman" 2 *Country Surveys*, 182 (1983).
72. *Ibid.*
73. *Ibid.*
74. Gerald E. Caiden, "International Handbook of the Ombudsman" 2 *Country Surveys*, 184 (1983).
75. *Ibid.*
76. Gerald E. Caiden, "International Handbook of the Ombudsman" 2 *Country Surveys*, 184 (1983).
77. *Ibid.*
78. *Ibid.*
79. *Ibid.*
80. *Ibid.*
81. D.R. Saxena, *Ombudsman(Lokpal): redress of citizens Grievances in India,* 50 (Deep and Deep Publications, New Delhi, 1987).
82. *Ibid.*
83. *Ibid.*
84. *Ibid.*
85. *Ibid.*

86. D.R. Saxena, *Ombudsman (Lokpal): redress of citizens Grievances in India,* 53 (Deep and Deep Publications, New Delhi, 1987).
87. *Ibid.*
88. *Ibid.*
89. *Ibid.*
90. D.R. Saxena, *Ombudsman (Lokpal): redress of citizens Grievances in India,* 57 (Deep and Deep Publications, New Delhi, 1987).
91. *Ibid.*
92. *Ibid.*
93. *Ibid.*
94. *Ibid.*
95. Donald C Rowat (ed.), *'The Ombudsmans* 25 (Grorge Allen & Unwin Ltd., London, 1968).
96. The judges themselves are Civil Servants, subject to being prosecuted for their carelessness and ignorance.
97. Lower civil servants may be prosecuted in Courts of First Instance:
    (i) The judges of the Courts along with superior civil servants and the heads of most Administrative Boards are triable in a court of Appeals.
    (ii) Appeals Court and heads of a few Central Administrative Boards are triable before the supreme court.
    (iii) Ministers and Members of the Supreme Court are triable before Special Court of Impeachment.
98. *Ibid.*
99. D.R. Saxena, *Ombudsman(Lokpal): redress of citizens Grievances in India,* 133 (Deep and Deep Publications, New Delhi, 1987).
100. *Ibid.*
101. Frank Stacey, *Ombudsman Compared'* 122 (Oxford, London, 1978).
102. M.P. Jain, *Lokpal: Ombudsman in India* 46 (Academic Books Limited, New Delhi, 1st edn., 1970).
103. *Ibid.*
104. *Ibid.*
105. *Ibid.*
106. *Ibid.*
107. D.R. Saxena, *Ombudsman (Lokpal): redress of citizensGrievances in India,* 150 (Deep and Deep Publications, New Delhi, 1987).
108. M.P. Jain, *Lokpal: Ombudsman in India* 67 (Academic Books Limited, New Delhi, 1st edn., 1970).

109. D. R. Saxena, *Ombudsman (Lokpal): redress of citizens Grievances in India,* 151 (Deep and Deep Publications, New Delhi, 1987).
110. *Ibid.*
111. D.R. Saxena, *Ombudsman (Lokpal): redress of citizens Grievances in India,* 152 (Deep and Deep Publications, New Delhi, 1987).
112. *Ibid.*
113. *Ibid.*
114. *Ibid.*
115. *Ibid.*
116. *Ibid.*
117. M.P. Jain, *Lokpal: Ombudsman in India* 81 (Academic Books Limited, New Delhi, 1st edn., 1970).
118. *Ibid.*
119. *Ibid.*
120. *Ibid.*
121. *Ibid.*
122. *Ibid.*
123. *Ibid.*
124. *Ibid.*
125. *Ibid.*
126. *Ibid.*
127. *Ibid.*
128. *Ibid.*
129. *Ibid.*
130. *Ibid.*
131. *Ibid.*
132. *Ibid.*
133. Section 3 of the The Lokpal and Lokayuktas Act, 2013.
134. Section 3 of the The Lokpal and Lokayuktas Act, 2013.
135. Section 25 of the Lokpal and Lokayuktas Act, 2013.
136. Section 27 of the Lokpal and Lokayuktas Act, 2013.
137. Section 34 of the Lokpal and Lokayuktas Act, 2013.
138. Section 14 of 'The Lokpal and Lokayuktas Act, 2013'.
139. Section 2(e) of the Lokpal and Lokayuktas Act, 2013.
140. Section 20 of 'The Lokpal and Lokayuktas Act, 2013'.

Chapter 4

A Critical Appraisal of the Lokpal and Lokayuktas Act, 2013

"When the people fear the government, there is tyranny. When the government fears the people, there is liberty."[1]

Before the Lokpal and Lokayuktas Act, 2013, public servants (such as government employees, judges, armed forces, police) could be prosecuted for corruption under the Indian Penal Code, 1860 and the Prevention of Corruption Act, 1988. However, the Code of the Criminal Procedure required the investigating agency (such as CBI) to get prior sanction of the Central or state Government before it could initiate the prosecution process in a court.[2] This mandatory provision questions the working of the CBI independently. Every now and then, there have been controvercies regarding the same. The Supreme Court in the "Coalgate Scam"[3] characterised the CBI as 'a caged parrot speaking its masters' voice- "one parrot with many masters".

The authorities like CBI, CVC and ACB involved in inquiring, investigating and prosecuting corruption cases to address the issue of the corruption failed. The following tables have shown datas where the government has delayed sanction for officials so the Table No.5 shows the requests pending with the government.

4.1 Table No. 6

Requests for prosecution sanction pending with the Government[4]

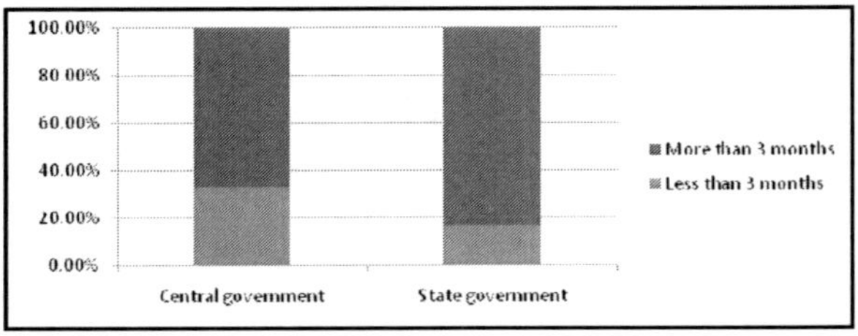

Prosecution of public servants can be taken up only after the concerned government gives sanction to do so. This provision was with the object to protect honest officials from harassment. However, the provision may be misused resulting into delaying response to requests for sanction.

i. By the end-2010, the central government had not provided any response to 236 requests. Of these, 155 requests (66 per cent) were pending for over three months.[5]

ii. The State government had not responded to 84 requests, of which 13(15 per cent) were pending for more than three months.[6] Since Central Vigilance Commission is also one of the agencies to address the corruption issue, it is equally important to see its position in this regard.

4.2 Table No. 7

The whistleblower mechanism has received only a few hundred complaints every year[7]

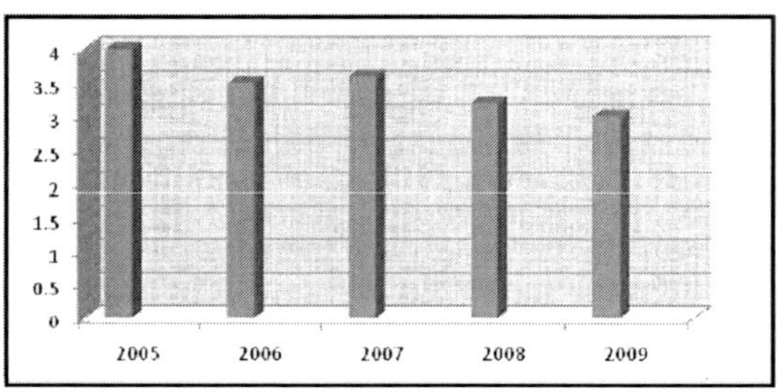

From the year 2005–2009, the Central Vigilance Commission received a total of 1, 731 complaints an annual average of 346.[8]

4.3 Table No. 8

Penalties imposed [in pursuance of Central Vigilance Commission (CVC)][9]

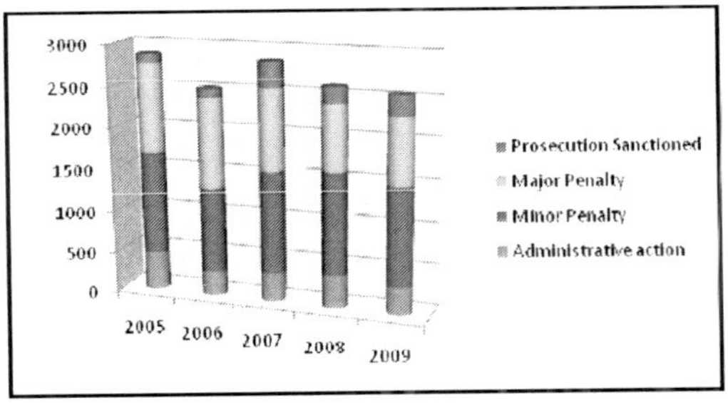

As discussed in the Chapter 1,

i. Between 2005-2009, penalties were imposed on 13, 061 cases based on CVC's advice.[10]

ii. 6 per cent of the cases were taken up for prosecution, and 94 per cent were given departmental penalties.[11]

iii. Major penalties were included in 4895 cases which includes, dismissal, reduction to lower rank, cut in pension etc.[12]

iv. Minor penalties were imposed on 5356 cases and administrative action was taken in 1964 cases.[13]

Table No. 9

The Courts have also been slow in deciding Central Vigilance Commission cases[14]

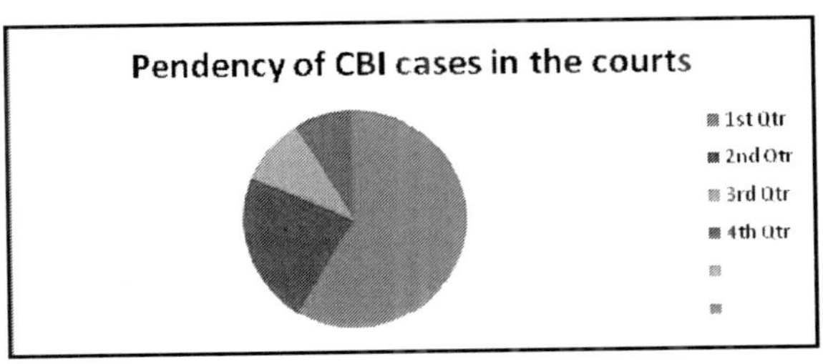

The Courts has also been slow in prosecuting the CBI cases.

i. By the end of the year 2010, there were 9, 927 CBI cases pending in courts.[15]

ii. And out of 9, 927, 2, 245 cases were pending for more than 10 years.[16]

Above mentioned data indicates that whether it is CBI or CVC whose primary task is to address and curb the corruption have not been able to successfully deal with it. So the need to have a mechanism to deal with the grievances of the citizen's was felt and to have an institution which can effectively curb the menace of corruption, an anti-corruption law 'The Lokpal and Lokayuktas Act, 2013 was passed by the Parliament which seeks to provide for the establishment of the institution of Lokpal and Lokayuktas to inquire into allegations of corruption against certain public functionaries and for matters connecting them.

However from the very passage of the Lokpal and Lokayuktas Act, 2013, there have been issues from the selection committe to the search committee formed under the Act.

The author doubts the anti corruption law, will completely eradicate the corruption from the country, so he is trying to highlight some issues which may answer the question of the working of the Lokpal independently and effectively.

4.5 Issue No 1. Invisible Constitutional Amendment[17]

4.5.1 Restriction on employment by Chairperson and Members after ceasing to hold office[18]

(1) On ceasing to hold office, the Chairperson and every Member shall be ineligible for—

(i) Reappointment as the Chairperson or a Member of the Lokpal;

(ii) Any diplomatic assignment, appointment as a administrator of a Union Territory and such other assignment or appointment which is required by law to be made by the President by warrant under his hand and seal;

(iii) Further employment to any other office of profit under the Government of India of the Government of the state;

(iv) Contesting any election of President or Vice President or Member of either House of Parliament or Member of either House of a state Legislature or Municipality or Panchayat within a period of five years from the date of relinquishing the post.

(2) Notwithstanding anything contained in sub-section (1), a Member shall be eligible to be appointed as the Chairperson, if his total tenure as Member and Chairperson does not exceed five years.

Explanation – For the purposes of this section, it is hereby clarified that where the Member is appointed as the Chairperson, his term of office shall not be more than five years in aggregate as the Member and the Chairperson. [Emphasis added]

It is provided that once a person has been in employment as the Chairperson or Member of the Lokpal, he is restricted to Contest any election of President or Vice President or Member of either House of Parliament or Member of either House of a state Legislature or Municipality or Panchayat within a period of five years from the date of relinquishing the post.[19] However no such additional qualification has been provided under the Constitution of India in which the qualifications have been given in Article 58.[20] Under the Constitution of India a person must have the following qualifications for the election as President:

4.5.2 Article 58[21]

Qualifications for election as President.—(1) No person shall be eligible for election as President unless he—

(a) is a citizen of India.

(b) has completed the age of thirty-five years, and

(c) is qualified for election as a member of the House of the People.

(2) A person shall not be eligible for election as President if he holds any office of profit under the Government of India or the Government of any State or under any local or other authority subject to the control of any of the said Governments.

Explanation.—for the purposes of this article, a person shall not be deemed to hold any office of profit by reason only that he is the President or Vice-President of the Union or the Governor of any State or is a Minister either for the Union or for any State.

The abovementioned qualifications have been specifically mentioned into the Constitution of India for the election as the President of India.

4.5.3 Comments

i. Section 8(iv) of the Act[22], will result into indirectly addition of one more qualification given under Article 58 of the Constitution of India for the election as the President of India. It will amount to encroach into the Constitution of India.

ii. It amounts to amendment to the constitution indirectly which may be termed as 'invisible constitutional amendment'[23] without amending the Constitution in any sense, thus, by passing the constitutional provision relating to amendment[24] and procedure[25] thereof.

4.6 Issue No 2. Will new section- 8B(2) of CVC Act dilute the powers of CBI?[26]

The Lokpal and Lokayuktas Act, 2013 also made amendments into the Central Vigilance Commission Act 2003.[27] The object of the Bill is to set up a Lokpal at the Centre and Lokayuktas in states by State law enacted by respective legislatures within one year of coming into force of the Act.[28] The Bill was first passed by the Lok Sabha in the winter session of 2011, but not by the Rajya Sabha, where it was debated and the house was adjourned before voting on it.[29] Later, the Rajya Sabha Select Committee had suggested changes in the Bill, most of which are incorporated in the present Act.[30]

The Lokpal can inquire into offences under the Prevention of Corruption Act, 1988 committed by seven persons who are as under;[31]

i. members of Parliament,

ii. group A and B government officials,

iii. employees of a company,

iv. society set up by an Act of Parliament or

v. a trust set up by an Act of Parliament, or

vi. society financed by the central government or

vii. Society controlled by the central government. However the insertion of some sections into the Central Vigilance Act, 2003 after the Lokpal and Lokayuktas Act, 2013 came into existence, was debated.

4.6.1 Insertion of new Sections 8A and 8B of the Central Vigilance Commission Act, 2003[32]—The newly incorporated Section 8B (2) of the Central Vigilance Commission Act has been a point of discussion and to under it better, we need to know the new inserted section 8A of CVC act.

Section 8A [33]*Action on preliminary inquiry in relation to public servants,* - (1) Where, after the conclusion of the preliminary inquiry relating to corruption of public servants belonging to Group C and Group D officials of the Central Government, the findings of the commission disclose, after giving an opportunity of being heard to the public servant, a prima facie violation of conduct rules relating to corruption under the Prevention of Corruption Act, 1988 (49 of 1988) by such public servant, the Commission shall proceed with one or more of the following actions, namely:—

(a) Cause an investigation by any agency or the Delhi Special Police Establishment, as the case may be;

(b) Initiation of the disciplinary proceedings or any other appropriate action against the concerned public servant by the competent authority;

(c) Closure of the proceedings against the public servant and to proceed the complainant under section 46 of the Lokpal and Lokayuktas Act, 2013.

(2) Every preliminary inquiry referred to in sub-section (1) shall ordinarily be completed within a period of ninety days and for reasons to be recorded in writing, within a further period of ninety days from the date of receipt of the complaint.

4.6.2 Section 8B. Action on investigation in relation to public servants[34]

(1) In Case the Commission decides to proceed to investigate into the complaint under clause (a) of sub-section (1) of section 8A, it shall direct any agency (including The Delhi Special Police Establishment) to carry out the investigation as expediously as possible and complete the investigation within a period of six months from the date of its order and submit the investigation report containing its finding to the commission : Provided that the Commission may extend the said period by a further period of six months for the reasons to be recorded in writing.

(2) Notwithstanding anything contained in section 173 of the Code of Criminal Procedure, 1973, any agency (including The Delhi Special Police Establishment) shall, in respect of cases referred to it by the commission.

(3) The Commission shall consider every report received by it under sub-section (2) from any agency (including The Delhi Special Police Establishment) and may decide as to –

(a) File charge sheet or closure report before the Special Court against the public servant;

(b) Initiate the departmental proceedings or any other action against the concerned public servant by the competent authority.

Which mandates that any agency (including the Delhi Special Police Establishment) shall submit the investigation report to the Central vigilance Commission, in respect of cases referred to it by the Central.[35]

4.6.3 Area of Concern[36]

Sections 8A and 8B of CVC Act deals with the inquiry and investigation relating to corruption of public servants belonging to Group C and Group D officials of the Central Government.[37] According to section 8A where, after the conclusion of the preliminary inquiry relating to corruption of public servants belonging to Group C and Group D officials of the Central Government, the findings of the Commission disclose, after giving an opportunity of being heard to the public servant, a prima facie violation of conduct rules relating to corruption under the Prevention of Corruption Act, 1988 by such public servant, the Commission shall proceed with one or more of the following actions, namely:[38]—

(a) Cause an investigation by any agency or the Delhi Special Police Establishment, as the case may be;

(b) Initiate disciplinary proceedings or any other appropriate action against the concerned public servant by the competent authority;

(c) Closure of the proceedings against the public servant and to proceed against the complainant under section 46 of the Lokpal and Lokayuktas Act, 2013.

As per Section 8B(1), in case the Commission decides to proceed to investigate into the complaint under clause (a) of sub-section (1) of section 8A, it shall direct any agency (including the Delhi Special Police Establishment) to carry out the investigation as expeditiously as possible and complete the investigation within a period of six months from the date of its order and submit the investigation report containing its findings to the Commission.[39] Sub-section 2 of section 8B mandates that *notwithstanding anything contained in section 173 of the Code of*

Criminal Procedure, 1973, any agency (including the Delhi Special Police Establishment) shall, in respect of cases referred to it by the Commission, ***submit the investigation report to the Commission.***[40] [Emphasis Added]

According to sub-section (3) of section 8B, the Commission shall consider every report received by it under sub-section (2) from any agency (including the Delhi Special Police Establishment) and may decide as to[41]—

(a) File charge-sheet or closure report before the Special Court against the public servant;[42]

(b) Initiate the departmental proceedings or any other appropriate action against the concerned public servant by the competent authority."[43]

Section 173 of Cr. PC which have been upheld by various courts in the country, an investigating officer shall file the final report only before competent magistrate but now the **new provision make it necessary to show it to CVC** as well which is a serious dilution of its powers.[44]

The very success of the investigation agency lies upon the independence of the agency. The independence of such institution has always been debated on the different forums. The Supreme Court has now and then stated the independence of it which could be observed in following cases.

In ***H.N. Rishbud and Inder Singh* v. *The State of Delhi***[45] a three Judge Bench of the Supreme Court, after delineating the different steps in investigation as contemplated in Cr.P.C, has pointed out that the formation of the opinion, whether or not there is a case to place the accused on trial, should be that of the officer in charge of the police station and none else.

In ***State* v. *Raj Kumar Jain***[46] a two judge bench considered the legality of an order passed by a Special Judge before whom the CBI filed final report in respect of a junior engineer who was pitted against offences under the Prevention of Corruption Act.

The CBI in the report held that the allegations made against him were unsubstantiated. But the Special Judge declined to accept the said report as in his opinion the CBI should have taken the view of the Sanctioning Authority. So the Special Judge directed the CBI to conduct further investigation after approaching the Sanctioning Authority. Though the High Court of Delhi did not interfere with the said direction, the Supreme Court interfered with it and observed as follows: [47]

> Viewed in that context, the CBI was under no obligation to place the materials collected during investigation before the sanctioning authority, when they found that no case was made out against the respondent. To put it differently, if the CBI had found on investigation that a prima facie case was made out against the respondent to place him on trial and accordingly prepared a charge-sheet (challan) against him, then only the question of obtaining sanction of the authority under section 6(1) of the Act would have arisen for without that the Court would not be competent to take cognisance of the charge-sheet. It must, therefore, be said that both the Special Judge and the High Court were patently wrong in observing that the CBI was required to obtain sanction from the prosecuting authority before approaching the Court for accepting the report under section 173(2) of Cr. PC for discharge of the respondent.[48]

In ***Sarala* v. *Velu***[49] the Apex Court while dealing with a case where in the investigation officer concerned was directed by the High Court to take back the case from the court (whereat it was laid by him after completing the investigation) and further directed to consult the Public Prosecutor and submit a fresh charge-sheet in tune with the opinion of the Public Prosecutor, after quoting the above Judgments, clarified that the formation of opinion in a case is the exclusive domain of the investigating officer and at any rate no investigating agency can be compelled to seek opinion of anybody including a Public Prosecutor even under the orders of court.[50]

4.6.4 Comments

i. Section 173 of Cr. PC which has been upheld by various courts in the country, an investigating officer shall file the final report only before competent magistrate but now the **new provision make it necessary to show it to CVC** which is a serious dilution of its powers.

ii. The issue required to be looked upon there has been instances when the court had already gone through situations where the Central Vigilance Commissioner himself was charge sheeted under the Prevention of Corruption Act.

iii. There is an element of ambiguity which required to be looked into by ensuring the independency of the Investigation agency must have clarity on the issue and, if necessary, make changes in the Lokpal and CVC Act accordingly.

4.7 Issue No. 3—Section 4(1)d & 4(1)e of Selection Committee under the Lokpal and Lokayuktas Act, 2013

Lokpal and Lokayukta Act, 2013 within a short span of its coming into force now become the subject matter of judicial review with respect to some issues which requires a serious consideration on the part of the government, failing which the country will fail to have a strong anti – corruption law which, we waited for decades. So here the author wants to address the issue of the appointment of by the selection committee under the Lokpal and Lokayuktas Act, 2013.

4.7.1 Appointment of Chairperson and Members on recommendations of Selection Committee[51]

(1) The chairperson and Members shall be appointed by the President after obtaining the recommendations of a Selection Committee consisting of –

(a) The Prime Minister – Chairperson.

(b) The speaker of the house of the people–Member;

(c) The leader of the opposition in the house of the people–Member;

***(d) The Chief Justice of India or a judge of the Supreme Court nominated by him- Member*;**

(e) One eminent jurist, as recommended by the Chairperson and members preferred to in clauses (a) to (d) above, to be nominated by the President- Member.[Emphasis added]

4.7.2 Section 4(1)d of the Lokpal and Lokayuktas Act, 2013 says that

> The Chief Justice of India or a judge of the Supreme Court of India nominated by the Chief Justice of India will be one of the members of the selection committee who will recommend the Chairman and the members of the Lokpal, such function of judiciary will result into participation of the judiciary in the executive function, which will may result into compromising the independence of the Judiciary. The author's view finds the place under the challenge of the Constitutionality of Section 4(1)d of the Lokpal and Lokayuktas Act, 2013 before the High Court of Kerala[52] the participation of the Chief Justice of India or his nominee in the selection committee constituted for the purpose of appointing Chairperson and members of the Lokpal when the provision enables the appointment of the Chief Justice of India and judges of the Supreme Court of India themselves, as Chairperson and members of the Lokpal, will vitiate the selection and appointment process apart from being against law as bias is writ large in such an appointment by the Committee thereby rendering Section 4(1)(d) of the Lokpal and Lokayuktas Act, 2014, unconstitutional.[53]

A writ petition[54] has been filed by Sri. P. Subair Kunju challenging the constitutional validity of certain provisions of the Central Act, 1 of 2014 (Lokpal and Lokayuktas Act, 2014). On the ground that these provisions will *'in effect result in unintentional participation of the judiciary in the executive function, which will have far reaching ramification and negative impact insofar as the independence of the judiciary is concerned'.*[55] [Emphasis added]

It was contended on behalf of the Petitioner that the inclusion of the Chief Justice of India or his nominee in the Selection Committee is a conscious attempt to make the judiciary a part of the executive function, as the legislation passed is without due deliberations on all aspects by the parliament and the consequences attached to such a process, and that the inclusion of the Chief Justice of India or his nominee, by itself in the Selection Committee will not make the appointment or the appointee a *'holy cow'*.[56]

It pointed out that at least four sitting judges of the Supreme Court "are reported to have expressed their willingness for being considered for the post of judicial member of the Lokpal. Their candidature even though permitted under section 3 of the Act[57], will seriously compromise the independence of the judiciary which is a part of the basic feature of our constitution.

The petitioner criticised who has/have furnished his or her bio-data on their own to the Search Committee or the Selection Committee for being considered for appointment, and seeks a declaration from the High Court that *'any person including the serving Chief Justice of India or serving judges of the Supreme Court of India if had given their curriculum vitae to be scrutinized by the search committee or the selection committee, they cannot be considered as persons of eminence and they cannot discharge their constitutional function in terms of the oath which they have taken and decide matters in relation to the Union while they are awaiting an appointment by the Executive.'*[58] [Emphasis Added]

The petitioner further seeks a declaration that the constitution of the search committee in preparing the panel of persons and the functions to be performed by the Search Committee in identifying persons to be considered by the selection committee which includes the serving Chief Justice of India and judges of the Supreme Court of India is unconstitutional;[59]

> for a writ of mandamus directing the Union Government not to constitute the selection committee with the Chief Justice of India or his nominee as a member in the selection committee for appointment to the post of Chairperson and Member of Lokpal as provided for in Sections of the Act[60], and also for a writ, order or direction from the High Court of Kerala, restraining the Search Committee in considering the curriculum vitae of serving judges of the Supreme Court while preparing the panel for consideration by the selection committee as provided under sub-section (3) of section 4.[61] It was pointed out that the four members of the selection committee had not met. The search committee rules have thus been framed even though the selection committee had not even been constituted on January 17, the petitioner said.

The power of framing the rules and regulations can be done only with the approval of the selection committee under section 4(4) of the Act[62]. In this background, the whole process of framing the search committee rules and inviting application by the ministry is contrary to the provisions of the Act and liable to set aside. He further said that the rules have contained various unwanted things including classifying the applicants, seeking recommendation letter from eminent people associated with vigilance and anti-corruption etc., which were not actually told in the Act. Rule 10 of the search committee rules[63] is contrary to and ultra vires the provisions of section 3(3)(b) and 3(4) of the Act[64]. Under section 3(3) of the Act,[65] people of outstanding ability from different fields are eligible to be appointed as non-judicial members.

But Rule 10 stipulates that only those who have held the post of secretary to the central and state governments are eligible to become members of the Lokpal and as per another rule, only those holding the post of Chairman, Managing Director or CEO of a public sector undertaking can be eligible to become non-judicial members of the Lokpal.[66]

The Petitioner further said that there are no guidelines as to the basis on which the selection committee will select one out of the five names recommended for the post of chairperson of the Lokpal and eight of 24 names recommended for the post of members of the Lokpal. He said that "In fact, it is mandatory for the selection committee to frame guidelines before search committee rules can be framed, " Though the petitioner had, as an interim relief, sought for an order restraining the Search Committee from considering the curriculum vitae of any serving judge of the Supreme Court for the post of Chairperson or member of the Lokpal and submitting their names to the selection committee, pending disposal of the Writ Petition, the High Court did not pass any interim orders in the case.[67]

4.7.3 Comments

i. The participation of the Chief Justice of India or his nominee in the selection committee constituted for the purpose of appointing Chairperson and members of the Lokpal when the provision enables the appointment of the Chief Justice of India and judges of the Supreme Court of India themselves, as Chairperson and members of the Lokpal, will vitiate the selection and appointment process apart from being against law as bias.

ii. The requirement that an individual should apply to the DoPT (Department of Personnel and Trainning) to prove his interest and credentials for being appointed to the Lokpal or to its group of eight seems obnoxious. We want individuals who will not seek this job but who are persuaded to take it up out of a commitment to the nation. They should be those who are viewed by an objective group led by the Prime Minister as eminently suitable both from competence and integrity points of view. This course of action will eliminate pompous and greedy elements in society who wish to trespass into a territory where only legally sharp minds and those have a track record for honesty and public spirit are welcome.

iii. Once the search panel arrives at suitable and cridible names, the selection panel may have to spend very little time drawing up the final list.

4.7.4 Section 4(1)(e) of the Lokpal and Lokayuktas Act, 2013

Section 4(e) of the Act[68] has been a point of debate from the very existence of the Lokpal and Lokayuktas Act, 2013. Selection Committee comprises of a chairperson and four other members which will recommend the chairperson and other members of the Lokpal and the President of India will appoint them. Here the resercher tries to highlight the problem with the Section 4(e) of the Act[69] which says that—

> *"One eminent jurist, as recommended by the Chairperson and members preferred to in clauses (a) to (d) above, to be nominated by the President- Member"*[70] [Emphasis added].

As per section 4(a) and 4(b) of the Lokpal and Lokayuktas Act, 2013, there will the Prime Minister as the chairperson and the Speaker of the House of the People as member of the Selection Committee.[71] From the other members, one will be a member who will be the leader of the opposition and the other member will be the chief justice of India or a judge of the Supreme Court nominated by him as the member of the Selection Committee.[72]

Regarding the appointment of the fifth member by the recommendation of the chairperson and members referred from section 4(a-d), there is a clear chance of the majority rule winning in favour of the government's opinion as there are two members section 4(a) and section 4(b) who will be from the government.

The idea of the government majority rule will in most of the cases will prevail and the government's say in the selection of the fifth member can not be ruled out at most of the time. The author's doubt about the appointment by the selection, finds the way in the following issues raised by the leaders of the opposition. Ms Sushma Swaraj the leader of the opposition in Lok sabha had proposed the name of eminent jurist K. Parasaran, but the panel did not agree. She then suggested that the meeting should either be deffered or the panel should be extended to include more names or the name should be picked through consensus, not majority vote. None of these suggestions was accepted and it was put on record that the name was picked on 3:1 majority.[73]

There was confrontation over the choice of senior advocate P.P. Rao on the selection panel is set to reach the doorstep of President Pranab Mukherjee, with the BJP deciding to seek his intervention.[74] So author wants to discuss about the majority and consensus vote.

4.7.4.1 Majority Rule

According to *Webster's Ninth New Collegiate Dictionary*

A political principal providing that a majority constituted by fifty percent plus one of an organised group will have the power to make decisions binding upon the whole.[75] Majority rule is a decision rule that selects alternatives which have a majority that is more that half the votes. It is the binary decision rule used most often in influential decision-making bodies, including the legislatures of democratic nations.

4.7.4.2 Consensus

According to *The Macquarie Dictionary*

1. General agreement or concord. 2. Majority of opinion.[76]

Consesus decision – making is a group decision making process that consent of all participants.

4.7.5 Comments

Majority rule, as per the selection committe under section 4(e) of the Lokpal and Lokpayukta Act, 2013 requires the consent of more than fifty percent (i.e consent of 3 members out of the 5) to reach at the decision for the appointment of the fifth member, One eminent jurist, as recommended by the Chairperson and members preferred to in clauses (a) to (d) of the section 4 of the Act, to be nominated by the President—as member of the Selection Committee.

i. Consensus rule however makes it mandatory to have consent of all the members of the Committee to reach at a particular decision.

ii. Here loking at the importance of the Selection Committee for the recommendations of names of the Chairperson and the members for the appointment by the President in the Lokpal, it is required that the selection committee should act fairly and with integrity. The opinion of very member must be taken into consideration so having a consensus while appointing the 5th member will lead to end in fruitful result.

4.8 Issue No. 4 The Search Committee under section 4(3) of the Lokpal and Lokayuktas Act, 2013 and Rule 10(1) of the Search Committee Rules, 2014.

There has been discussion over the conflictions between the Search Committee under the Act and search committee rules, which can be observed by the eminent jurists taking their names from the Search Committee under the section 4(3) of the Act. So it becomes important to study the Section 4(3) of the Lokpal and Lokayuktas Act, 2013 and rule 10(1) of the Search Committee Rules, 2014.

4.8.1 Section 4(3) of the Lokpal and Lokayuktas Act, 2013[77]

The Selection Committee shall for the purposes of selecting the Chairperson and Members of the Lokpal and for preparing a panel of persons to be considered for appointment as such, constitute a search committee consisting of at least seven persons of standing and having special knowledge and expertise in the matters relating to anti-corruption policy, public administration, vigilance, policy making, finance, including insurance and banking, law and management or in any other matter which, in the opinion of the selection Committee, may be useful in making the selection of the Chairperson and Members of the Lokpal:

> Provided that not less than fifty per cent of the members of the Search Committee shall be from amongst the persons belonging to the Scheduled Castes, the Scheduled Tribes, other Backward Classes, Minorities and women: Provided further that Selection Committee may also consider any person other than the persons recommended by the Search Committee.

4.8.2 Rule 10(1)[78] of the Search Committee Rules, 2014 says that:

> The Search Committee shall prepare a panel of persons to be considered by the selection committee for appointment as the Chairperson and Members of the Lokpal, from amongst the list of persons provided by the Central Government in the Department of Personnel and Training.[79]

The process of putting in place an independent anti-corruption ombudsman has been in controvercy, exposing the government to the charge that it is in an unseemly hurry to appoint the body before the expiry of its term.[80] There is anomaly in the Lokpal Act and the rules framed under it.

The Act says: "………..Persons chosen for search Committee should have special knowledge and expertise in the matters relating to anti-corruption policy, public administration, vigilance, policy making, finance including insurance and banking, law and management or in any other matter."

However, the Rules[81] prescribe that such persons must have expertise in the field for at least 25 years.[82]The Section 61 of the Act[83] says,

> *"Every rule and regulation made under this Act shall be laid before each House of Parliament, while it is in session, for*

30 days which may be comprised in one session or in two or more successive sessions." for ratification

But that had not happened.[84] Such kind of confliction between the The Lokpal and Lokayuktas Act, 2013 and the Search Committee Rules, 2014, from the beginning led to challenge the Search Committee Rule.

4.8.3 Judicial Review of the Search Committee Rule

The constitutionality of Search Committee Rules, 2014 has come under challenge in two separate Public Interest Litigations- one before the Supreme Court[85] and the other, before the Madurai bench of the Madras High Court.[86]

In a writ petition, Common cause said, "the Rule, in so far as it provides that the Search Committee shall prepare a panel of persons to be considered by the Selection Committee for appointment of the chairperson and members of the Lokpal from amongst the list provided by the Central Government. It was pointed out by the petitioner that such process directly runs counter to the very object of having an independent Lokpal and the Provisions of the said Act."[87]

The process involves a Selection Committee that will appoint a search committee. Going by the rules the search panel will scrutinise only applications forwarded to it by the Department of Personnel and Training.[88] The rules circumscribes the search committee's role to chosing names out of a list submitted by the government and blocks any independent nomination from the community at large. Further, the panel of names recommended by it need not be accepted by the Selection Committee, which is free to consider names from the outside the panel too. [89]

Such being the working of search committee under the act, has beed debated and critisised by many jurists. Justice K.T. Thomas, formerly of the Supreme Court, who was to head the search panel, and Fali Nariman, an eminent lawyer chosen to be a part of the panel, were quick to comprehend that their role was purely clerical.[90] What Justice Thomas and the others were asked to do was something that could have been done effortlessly by a DoPT Section Officer.[91]

Justice K.T. Thomas went through the rules framed under the Lokpal and Lokayuktas act and noted that the Search Committee's recommendations were not binding the selection committee headed by the Prime Minister.[92]

So he pointed out that in this case we have been burdened with two Panels – a search panel and a selection panel to appoint ombudsman.[93] On the face of it, this seems like needless complication.[94] The objective of the Department of Personnel and Training (DoPT) was perhaps to lighten the load of the Selection Committee. This was unexceptionable, but only to an extent.[95]

The petitioner said "Rule[96], *which states that non-judicial members of the Lokpal, apart from having special knowledge and expertise of not less than 25 years in matters relating to the anti-corruption policy, public administration, vigilance or law, must have held or must be holding the post of Secretary to the Government of India or any equivalent thereto under the Central Government or a State government travels beyond the scope of the Lokpal Act*". [Emphasis added]

> The petitioner has challenged the Search Committee (constitution, terms and conditions of appointment of members and the manner of selection of panel of names for appointment of chairperson and members of Lokpal) Rules, 2014 on the ground that it is contrary to the provisions of the Lokpal and Lokayuktas Act, 2014 and ultra vires Article 14 of the Constitution of India.[97] The petitioner has further sought a ban on the search committee to recommend the panel of names to the selection committee to select a Lokpal and its members.[98]

4.8.4 Comments

i. When the much delayed Bill was passed in Parliament in December 2013, there was a sense of relief that a reasonably sound law was in place. However, the government equipped itself with some potential filters while framing the rules.

ii. Empowering the apex committee with the freedom to go beyond the recommendations may not be inherently wrong. However, the potential for mischief in confining the first stage to a government mist and conferring wide discretion on the selection panel in the second stage may ultimately result in some deserving candidates being ignored or worse someone deemed inconvenient being disregarded. The need is for a transparent and credible selection system. The Government is required to save the credibility of the process; as an immediate step, it should revisit the rules and give a free hand to the search committee to do its job.

iii. What is required is freedom for the search panel to draw up its recommendations instead of being held hastage to what the DoPT places before them. This is as much transparency as we can expect in the present times, marked by venality and partisanship.

4.9 Issue No. 5 CONSTITUTIONAL STATUS OF LOKPAL

India is committed to pursue the policy of 'Zero Tolerance against Corruption'. India ratified the United Nations Convention against Corruption in 2003 by deposit of Instrument of Ratification on 9th May, 2011.[99]

This Convention imposes a number of obligations, some mandatory, some recommendatory and some optional on the Member States. The Convention, inter alia, envisages that State Parties ensure measures in the domestic law for criminalisation of offences relating to bribery and put in place an effective mechanism for its enforcement.[100]

The obligations of the Convention, with reference to India, have come in to force with effect from 8th June, 2011.[101] As a policy of Zero Tolerance against Corruption the Bill seeks to establish, in the country, a more effective mechanism to receive complaints relating to allegations of corruption against public servants includ-ing Ministers, MP's, Chief Ministers, Members of Legislative Assemblies and Public servants and to inquire into them and take follow up actions.[102] The bodies, namely, Lokpal and Lokayuktas which are being set up for the purpose will be *Constitutional Bodies*.[103] This setting up of these bodies will further strengthen the existing legal and institutional mechanism thereby facilitating a more effective implementation of some of the obligations under the aforesaid Convention.[104]

The Department Related Parliamentary Standing Committee on Personnel, Public Grievances, Law and Justice on the 8th August, 2011 recommended that Lokpal at the Centre and Lokayukta at the States be conferred *Constitutional Status* in its report of 9th December, 2011. Up on the recommendation of the Committee it was decided to withdraw the Lokpal Bill, 2011 pending in Lok Sabha and to introduce a throughly revised bill for carrying out the necessary amendments to the Constitution for the setting up of Lokpal and Lokayuktas as *Constitutional Status*.[105] It was recommended by The Department Related Parliamentary Standing Committee that the Lokpal at the centre and the Lokayuktas at the state be conferred Constitutional Status.[106] However, the Lokpal and Lokayuktas Bill, 2013 was passed by the Rajya Sabha on 17th December, 2013 after making certain amendments to the earlier Bill and in the Lok Sabha on 18th December, 2013.[107]

The very Introductory Chapter and the statement of object and reasons of the Lokpal and Lokayuktas Act, 2013 states that the Lokapal at the centre and the Lokayuktas at the states be conferred the Constitutional Status.[108]

However, the said act was passed by the Parliament by simple majority and without giving it any constitutional status. It seems that the legislation passed is without due deliberations on all aspects by the parliament and the consequences attached to such a process which may have a far reaching impact, must be looked upon sincerely and necessary amendment must be made. The reasons behind giving any institution constitutional status is its independence, making it efficient, working smoothly, and if any changes is required to be made, it should be done with a debate in to the parliament, requiring an amendment to the constitution. The Vigilance Commissions have mainly investigated into the complaints against petty officials, and being a sort of government department do not entertain grievances regarding maladministration involving high officials and Ministers. These Commissions do not enjoy a constitutional status and therefore there is no wonder if they have failed to give relief against those who control the government.[109]

The Procedure for amendment is—

An amendment of the constitution may be initiated only by the introduction of a Bill for the purpose in either House of the Parliament, and when the Bill is passed in each house by a majority (i.e., more than 50 per cent) of the total membership of that house and by a majority of not less than two-thirds of the members of that House present and voting, it shall be presented to the President for his assent and upon such assent being given to the Bill, the Constitution shall stand amended in accordance with the terms of the Bill.

It would be pointed out that there is important point on which the passage of a Constitution amendment Bill differs from the procedure relating to the passage of a Bill for ordinary legislation.

4.9.1 Advantages of the Lokpal as a Constitutional Body[110]

The institution of the Lokpal should be a constitutional body like the Election Commission or the Comptroller & Auditor

General, which has the status of a judge of Supreme Court.[111] It would have be advantageous if the Lokpal institution should have been made a constitutional body rather than a mere statutory authority.[112] Any change in the structure or status of a mere statutory authority can be made by a simple majority in the legislature enacting an ordinary legislation, whereas such a change in a constitutional body would require a constitutional amendment adhering to the principle of federalism.[113] No doubt the initial creation of the Lokpal as a constitutional body would itself require a constitutional amendment but that will suffice the demand of the 'strong Lokpal'.[114] Corruption free governance is a basic human right, more so in a developing country. In India it is a judicially recognised enforceable right derived from guaranteed fundamental rights.[115] The Human Development Report, 1999 on the theme of 'Crisis of Governance in South Asia', identified corruption as major cause for that crisis.[116]

A 'Strong Lokpal' to combat the malaise of corruption is a clarion call of the nation; and it is also a mean to address the constitutional promise made on the directive principle of state policy as well as eradication of poverty.[117] Corruption deepens poverty; it debases human rights, it degrades the environment; it derails development and it destroys confidence in democracy and the legitimacy of governments.[118] It debases human dignity. A constitutional Lokpal will be more effective to achieve this objective.[119]

Constitutional Lokpal to combat corruption would be to make its function a basic feature of the Constitution, and therefore, a part of its indestructible basic structure that would be beyond even the amending power under Article 368.[120] Immunity from vagaries of changing political equations in the era of coalitions is another benefit.[121] It is found that the constitutional bodies are comparatively more effective and immune from political and other extraneous influences than statutory bodies.[122] The need for creation of a 'Strong Lokpal' providing greater public confidence in its credibility is sufficient reason to prefer its constitutional status.[123]

4.9.2 Comments

i. Lokpal under the Lokpal and Lokayuktas Act, 2013 should be made constitutional, which will result in, it becoming more effective than statutory bodies.

ii. Lokpal under the Act once made a constitutional body can not be easily changed, without an amendment into the constitution, which is a difficult process.

References

1. Thomas Jefferson, the principal author of the Declaration of Independence (1776) and the third President of the United States (1801–1809).
2. Section 197 of the Code of Criminal Procedure and Section 19 of the Prevention of Corruption Act, 1988.
3.
4. *Supra* note 16.
5. *Ibid.*
6. *Ibid.*
7. Corruption cases against government officials, Number of Complaints received by CVC), India, *available at*: *http://www.prsindia.org/administrator/uploads/general/1302269425~~Vital%20Stats%20-%20Corruption%20cases%20against%20government%20officials%2008Apr11.pdf (Visited* on February 13, 2014).
8. *Ibid.*
9. Corruption cases against government officials, Penalties imposed (in pursuance of CVC's advice), India, *available at*: *http://www.prsindia.org/administrator/uploads/general/1302269425~~Vital%20Stats%20-%20Corruption%20cases%20against%20government%20officials%2008Apr11.pdf* (Visited on February 13, 2014).
10. Ibid.
11. Ibid.
12. Ibid.
13. Ibid.
14. Corruption cases against government officials, (The courts have been slow in deciding CBI cases), India, *available at*: *http://www.prsindia.org/administrator/uploads/general/1302269425~~Vital%20Stats%20-%20Corruption%20cases%20against%20government%20officials%2008Apr11.pdf(Visited* on February 13, 2014).

15. *Ibid.*
16. *Ibid.*
17. As I borrow the expression 'invisible constitutional amendment' from the celebrated work of Lawrence H. Tribe See, Lawrence H. Tribe, 'Invisible Constitution', Oxford University Press,
18. Section 8 of the Lokpal and Lokayuktas Act, 2013.
19. *Ibid.*
20. Article 58 of the Constitution of India.
21. *Ibid.*
22. Sec 8(iv) of the Lokpal and Lokayuktas Act, 2013.
23. As I borrow the expression 'invisible constitutional amendment' from the celebrated work of Lawrence H. Tribe. See, Lawrence H. Tribe, 'Invisible Constitution', Oxford University Press,
24. Article, 368
25. An Amendment to Article, 58 requires special provision and special majority as it falls under Part.
26. *available at http://www.livelaw.in/the-lokpal-and-lokayuktas-bill-2013-is-act-no-1-of-2014-will-new-section-8b2-of-cvc-act-dilute-the-powers-of-cbi/(visited* on 06/03/2014).
27. I. Commission of Inquiry Act, 1952,
    II. Delhi Police Establishment Act, 1946,
    III. Prevention of Corruption Act, 1988,
    IV. Code of Criminal Procedure, 1973 and
28. *Ibid.*
29. *Ibid.*
30. *Ibid.*
31. *Ibid.*
32. The Lokpal and Lokayuktas Act, 2013. p 33.
33. Section 8A of the Central Vigilance Commission Act, 2003.
34. Section 8B(1) Central Vigilance Commission Act, 2003.
35. *Ibid.*
36. Will new section- 8B(2) of CVC Act dilute the powers of CBI?, India, *availble* at:*http://www.livelaw.in/the-lokpal-and-lokayuktas-bill-2013-is-act-no-1-of-2014-will-new-section-8b2-of-cvc-act-dilute-the-powers-of-cbi/(Visited* on March 06, 2014).
37. *Ibid.*
38. *Ibid.*

39. *Ibid.*
40. *Ibid.*
41. *Ibid.*
42. *Ibid.*
43. *Ibid.*
44. *Ibid.*
45. *H.N. Rishbud and Inder Singh* v. *The State of Delhi* 1955 AIR 196 1955 SCR (1)1150.
46. *State* v. *Raj Kumar Jain* (1998) 6 SCC 551.
47. *Ibid.*
48. *State* v. *Raj Kumar Jain* (1998) 6 SCC 551.
49. (2002) *slp* (Cr.) 27 (11of 1999).
50. *Ibid.*
51. Section 4 the Lokpal and Lokayuktas Act, 2013
52. Constitutionality of setion 4(1)(d) of the Lokpal and Lokayuktas Act under challenge before the high court of Kerala, India, *available at: http://www.livelaw.in/constitutionality-section-41d-lokpal-lokayuktas-act-challenge-high-court-kerala/(Visited* on March 27, 2014).
53. *Ibid.*
54. W.P. (C) No. 4751 of 2014.
55. *Ibid.*
56. *Ibid.*
57. Section 3(3) of the Lokpal and Lokayuktas Act, 2013.
58. *Ibid.*
59. *Ibid.*
60. Section 4(1)(d) of the Central Act, 1 of 2014.
61. Sub-section (3) of section 4 of the Central Act, 1 of 2014 .
62. Section 4(4) of the Act of the Lokpal and Lokayukta Act, 2013.
63. Rule 10(4) of the Search Committee (Constitution, Terms, and conditions of appointment of members and the manner of selection of Panel of Names for appointment of Chairperson and Members of Lokpal) Rules, 2014.
64. Section 3(3)(b) and 3(4) of the Lokpal and Lokayukats Act, 2013.
65. Section 3(3) of the Act of the Lokpal and Lokayuktas Act, 2013.
66. Rule 10 of the Search Committee (Constitution, Terms, and conditions of appointment of members and the manner of selection of Panel of Names for appointment of Chairperson and Members of Lokpal) Rules, 2014.

67. *Ibid.*
68. Lokpal and Lokayuktas Act, 2013.
69. *Ibid.*
70. Section 4(e) of the Lokpal and Lokayuktas Act, 2013.
71. Section 4 of The Lokpal and Lokayuktas Act, 2013.
72. *Ibid.*
73. *Ibid.*
74. Smiriti Kak Ramachandran & Vinay Kumar, "The BJP and Government lock horns over Lokpal Selection Committee" *The Hindu,* Feb. 5, 2014.
75. *Webster's Ninth New Collegiate Dictionary,* 9th Edn., 718.
76. *The Macquarie Dictionary*, 1st Edn., p. 402.
77. The Lokpal and Lokayuktas Act, 2013.
78. Rule 10(1) of the Search Committee (Constitution, terms, and conditions of appointment of members and the manner of selection of Panel of Names for appointment of Chairperson and Members of Lokpal) Rules, 2014.
79. *Ibid.*
80. Editorial, "The Mischief in the rules" *The Hindu*, March 5, 2014.
81. Rule 10(4) of the Search Committee (Constitution, terms, and conditions of appointment of members and the manner of selection of Panel of Names for appointment of Chairperson and Members of Lokpal) Rules, 2014.
82. Editorial, "K.T. Thomas refuses to head Lokpal Search Panel", *The Hindu,* March 6, 2014.
83. Section 61 of the Lokpal and Lokayuktas Act, 2013.
84. *Ibid.*
85.
86. Lokpal: Constitutionality of 'Search Committee Rules, 2014 under challenge before the Supreme Court and Madras High Court, India, *available at:* http://www.livelaw.in/lokpal-constitutionality-search-committee-rules-2014-challenge-supreme-court-madras-high-court/ (Visited on March 06, 2014).
87. Editorial, "Rule falls foul of independent Lokpal: Plea", *The Hindu,* March. 05, 2014
88. *Ibid.*
89. *Ibid.*
90. *Ibid.*

91. *Ibid.*
92. *Ibid.*
93. R.K. Raghavan, "An exercise in futility?" *The Hindu,* March.7, 2014.
94. *Ibid.*
95. *Ibid.*
96. Rule 10(4)(i) of the Lokpal and Lokayuktas Act, 2013.
97. Constitutionality of section 4(1)(d) of the Lokpal and Lokayuktas Act under challenge before the High Court of Kerala, India, *available at: http://www.livelaw.in/constitutionality-section-41d-lokpal-lokayuktas-act-challenge-high-court-kerala/(Visited* on March 27, 2014).
98. *Ibid.*
99. The Lokpal and Lokayuktas Act, 2013.
100. *Ibid.*
101. *Ibid.*
102. *Ibid.*
103. *Ibid.*
104. *Ibid.*
105. *Ibid.*
106. *Ibid.*
107. *Ibid.*
108. *Ibid.*
109. D.R. Saxena, *Ombudsman(Lokpal): redress of citizens Grievances in India, 22* (Deep and Deep, New Delhi, 1987).
110. Advantages of the Lokpal as a Constitutional Body, India, a*vailable at :_https://indialawyers.wordpress.com/tag/rahul-gandhi/(Visited* on April 11, 2014).
111. *Ibid.*
112. *Ibid.*
113. *Ibid.*
114. *Ibid.*
115. *Ibid.*
116. Human Development report shows worsening poverty in South Asia, India, *available at:http://www.wsws.org/en/articles/1999/11/sasa-n29.html (Visited* on April 11, 2014).
117. Many advantages in Lokpal as a constitutional body, India, *available at:_https://indialawyers.wordpress.com/tag/rahul-gandhi/ (Visited* on April 11, 2014).

118. *Ibid.*
119. *Ibid.*
120. *Keshavananda Bharti* v. *State of Kerala* AIR 1973 SC 1461.
121. Many advantages in Lokpal as a constitutional body, India, *available at:_https://indialawyers.wordpress.com/tag/rahul-gandhi/ (Visited* on April 11, 2014).
122. *Ibid.*
123. *Ibid.*

Chapter 5

Conclusion

This chapter would cover the entire gamut of problem, the author wishes to highlight. He would like to admit that the whole journey from introduction of the grievance handling mechanism and its experience abroad, its acceptance by India and the issues which the he wishes to highlight has been very educative and informative.

5.1 Summary

The first chapter of the book started with the address to the issue of corruption and how it is drastically affecting the country. India is ranked amongst the most corrupt nations. The data has been shared to show the prime agencies involved in handling the issue of corruption have been failed.The Problem of the citizen's grievances had become accentuated in the past years as a result of several political, economic and social developments and a general deterioration in standards of administrative efficiency and integrity and the people's dissatisfaction with the administration grew substantially. So the reasearcher tried to find out why did these institutions fail? Which kind of mechanism, the country must have to address the grievances of its citizens. As the office of Ombudsman was adopted first by Sweden and it worked very effectively, it became equally important to study the historical aspect of this institution. So under the second chapter author has gone through the institutional development of the Ombudsman in different countries and in India. To understand better the office of the Ombudsman and its feasibility in India, he had compared the Ombudsman in Sweden, United Kingdom and India under the third chapter. Under the fourth chapter the author found some issues in 'The Lokpal and Lokayuktas Act, 2013' which has been highlighted.

5.2 Conclusion

'The Lokpal and Lokayuktas Act, 2013' was brought with the object to address the issue of corruption and to provide efficient, fair and inexpensive redressal of citizen's grievances which is one of the basic duties of government. However the author has highlighted some of the lacunas which required immediate attention. Section 8(iv) of the Lokpal and Lokayuktas Act, 2013 will result in to indirectly addition of one more qualification given under Article 58 of the Constitution of India for the election as the President of India. It will amount to encroach into the Constitution of India.The second issue is of insertion of new section 8B (2) of the Central Vigilance Commission which will dilute the powers of the Central Bureau of Investigation. The new inserted section of CVC mandates that any agency (including the Delhi Special Police Establishment) shall submit the investigation report to the Central Vigilance Commission in respect of cases referred to it by the Central, However in number of cases the Supreme Court and High Courts upheld section 173 of the Cr. PC that an investigating officer *shall* file the final report only before competent magistrate. It is further pointed out that section 4(1)(d) and 4(1)(e) of Selection Committee has been debated within a short span of the Lokpal Act coming into force. As per section 4(1)(d) of 'The Lokpal and Lokayuktas Act, 2013' the participation of the Chief Justice of India or his nominee in the Selection Committee and later their appointment as Chairperson and members of Lokpal will vitiate the selection and appointment process. Empowering the apex committee with the freedom to go beyond the recommendations may not be inherently wrong. However, the potential for mischief in confining the first stage to a government mist and conferring wide discretion on the selection panel in the second stage may ultimately result in some deserving candidates being ignored or worse someone deemed inconvenient being disregarded. Regarding the appointment of the fifth member by the recommendation of the chairperson and members referred from section 4(a-d) of the selection committee, there is a clear chance of the majority rule winning in favour of the government's opinion as there are two members section 4(a) and section 4(b) who will be from the government.There have been confliction in section 4(3) of 'The Lokpal and Lokayuktas Act, 2013' and Rule 10(1) of the Search Committee Rules, 2014. According to the former section the selection committee will constitute a search committee for preparing a panel of persons to be considered for appointment as Chairperson and Members of the Lokpal but it is not bound by the names suggested by the search committee which makes the search committee's recommendations not bounding upon the selection committee. However a per the later rule it appears that the search committee shall be bound to choose the names from the list of persons provided by the Central Government in the Department of Personnel and Trainning. The objective clause of 'The Lokpal and Lokayuktas Act, 2013' points out that the bodies, namely, Lokpal and Lokayuktas which are being set up for the purpose will be *Constitutional Bodies.*However the Act was passed by the Parliament by simple majority and without giving it any constitutional status. The author finally concludes here that in the absence of fairness in the selection of the Chairperson and Members of the Lokpal, it is difficult to say that the Lokpal constituted under the Present Lokpal Act will work without being dependent. His doubts about the constitutionality of certain provisions of 'The Lokpal and Lokayuktas Act, 2013' and Rules framed under the 'Search Committee Rules 2014', find its way, as the Act and Rules have been challenged into the Supreme Court and High Court of Kerala.

5.3 Ways a head

The author points out following ways a head:

i. Section 173 of Cr. PC which has been upheld by various courts in the country, an investigating officer shall file the final report only before competent magistrate but now the new provision make it necessary to show it to CVC which is a serious dilution of its powers.

ii. The issue required to be looked upon there has been instances when the court had already gone through situations where the Central Vigilance Commissioner himself was charge sheeted under the Prevention of Corruption Act.

iii. There is an element of ambiguity which required to be looked into by ensuring the independency of the Investigation agency must have clarity on the issue and, if necessary, make changes in the Lokpal and CVC Act accordingly.

iv. Majority rule, as per the selection committe under section 4(e) of the Lokpal and Lokayukta Act, 2013 requires the consent of more than fifty percent (i.e consent of 3 members out of the 5) to reach at the decision for the appointment of the fifth member, One eminent jurist, as recommended by the Chairperson and members preferred to in clauses (a) to (d) of the section 4 of the Act, to be nominated by the President- as member of the Selection–Committee.

v. Consensus rule however makes it mandatory to have consent of all the members of the Committee to reach at a particular decision.

vi. Here looking at the importance of the Selection Committee for the recommendations of names of the Chairperson and the members for the appointment by the President in the Lokpal, it is required that the selection committee should act fairly and with integrity. The opinion of very member must be taken into consideration so having a consensus while appointing the 5th member will lead to end in fruitful result.

vii. What is required is freedom for the search panel to draw up its recommendations instead of being held stage to what the DoPT places before them. This is as much transparency as we can expect in the present times, marked by venality and partisanship.

viii. Lokpal under the Lokpal and Lokayuktas Act, 2013 should be given constitutional status which will ensure it becoming more effective than statutory bodies.

Bibliography

(A) Primary Sources

Legislations and Codes

1. The Central Vigilance Commission Act, 2003 (45 of 2003).
2. The Criminal Procedure Code Act, 1973 (2 of 1974).
3. The Delhi Special Police Establishment Act, 1996 (25 of 1996).
4. The Indian Penal Code, 1860 (45 of 1860).
5. The Lokpal and Lokayuktas Act, 2013 (1 of 2014).
6. The Prevention of Corruption Act, 1988 (49 of 1988).

(B) Secondary Sources

(i) Books

Indian Authors

1. D. R. Saxena, *Ombudsman (Lokpal): Redress of citizens Grievances in India, 22* (Deep and Deep, New Delhi, 1987).
2. Girdhar B. Sharma, *Implementation of Ombudsman Plan in India* 6 (Ashish Publishing House, New Delhi, 1981).
3. Jagannadham and Makhija, "*Citizen's Administration and Lokpal*" 9 (S. Chand & Co., 1969).
4. M. Hidayatullah, "*Democracy in India and the Judicial Process*" 25 (Asia Publishing House, 1966).

5. M. P. Jain, *Lokpal: Ombudsman in India* 41 (Academic Books Limited, New Delhi, 1st edn., 1970).
6. R. K. Dhawan, *Public Grievances and the Lokpal* 165 (Allied Publishers Private Limited, New Delhi, 1st edn., 1981).
7. S. K. Agrawala, *Proposed Indian Ombudsmen : A Comparative Study of the Lokpal and Lokayukta Bill, 1968* (81 Agra, 1971).

Foreign Authors

1. Donald C. Rowat (ed.), *The Ombudsman* 7 (George Allen & Unwin Ltd., London, 1968).
2. Frank Stacey, *Ombudsman Compared'* 122 (Oxford, London, 1978).
3. Walter Gellhorn, *Ombudsmen and Others* 5 (Harvard University Press, Cambridge, 1967).

(ii) Articles/Journals

Indian Writers

1. Chandra Shekhar Joshi, "Need of Lokpal as Legal Instrument for Prevention of Corruption in India" 48, *Civil and Military Law Journal* 93 (2012).
2. Dr P.C Pati, "Corruption in India : Measures for its Prevention with reference to Prevention of Corruption Act, 1988" Vol. XXXI(3&4) *Indian Bar Review* 349 (2004).
3. Dr P. R. Dubhashi, "Independence of the CBI, Police and Administration", *Mainstream 19*(2013).
4. Lalit Uniyal, "People are not always right: why we do not need a super strong Lokpal", 50(6), *Mainstream,* 19-21 (2012).
5. M. C.J. Kargi, "Control of the Administration" *Public Law Journal*, 254-55 (1968).

6. Najmul Abedin, "Is the Jan Lokpal plan appropriate ? Conceptual and theoritical response to the question", 58(2), *Indian Journal of Public Administration* 197-215 (2012).
7. Norman Lewis and S. S. Singh "Citizen, Administration, and Ombudsman" in Norman Lewis, S. S. Singh et.al. (eds), *Ombudsman India and The World Community, 2* (1995).
8. P. B. Mukharji, "Grievance : Man in the Indian Administration System Ombudsman, Lokayukta and Lokpal", 17, *Indian Journal of Public Administration,* 408-24 (1971).
9. R. K. Swamy, "*The Case for a Permanent Tribunal of Inquiry*", Modern Review, 264, 1964.
10. S. Dutt, "Central Vigilance Commission and Lokpal", 17, *Journal of National Academy of Administration,* 13-20 (1972).
11. S. Jagerskiold, "The Swedish Constitution : A Survey" 5, *J.I.L.I* (1963).
12. S.L. Verma, "Lokpal, Bureaucracy and The Ccommon Man", 24, *Indian Journal of Public Administration,* 1130-44 (1978).
13. U.C. Agarwal, "Role of Lokpal in fostering Ethical Governance and Society" Vol LIX, No.*3 Indian Journal of Public Administration* 432 (2013).
14. U. P. D. Kesari, "Indian Lokpal: A Panacea of Administration Maladies", 19, *Journal of Lal Bahadur Sastry Academy of Administration* 281-89 (1974).

Foreign Writers

1. Bernard Frank, "The Ombudsman Revisited", *International Bar Journal* 55 (1975).

2. Donald C Rowat, *'Recent Development in Ombudsmanship. A review of Articles – Canadian Public Administration*, Vol.10. March 1967.
3. Gerald E. Caiden, "International Handbook of the Ombudsman" 2 *Country Surveys*, 179 (1983).
4. Joseph Minattur, "Ombudsman, Lokpal or Parliamentary Commissioner : Does custom state his infinite variety", 3, *Allahabad Law Review*, 29-43 (1971).
5. Joseph Ponnoly, "Dealing with maladministration. The need for Ombudsman in India", *C.B.I. Bulletin* 26 (1996).
6. Madam Justice Florence N.Mumba, "The Ombudsman: The need for Protection and Control" in Norman Lewis, S.S. Singh et.al. (eds), *Ombudsman India and The World Community*, 33 (1995).

(iii) Newspaper Articles

1. Editorial, "K.T. Thomas refuses to head Lokpal Search Panel", *The Hindu,* March 6, 2014.
2. Editorial, "The Mischief in the rules" *The Hindu*, March 5, 2014.
3. Smiriti Kak Ramachandran & Vinay Kumar, "The BJP and Government lock horns over Lokpal Selection Committee" *The Hindu,* February 5, 2014.
4. Sriram Panchu, "Repairing the Lokpal Bill", 47(3), *Economic and Political Weekly,* 10-13(2012).
5. R. K. Raghavan, "An exercise in futility?" *The Hindu,* March 7, 2014.

(iv) Reports

1. Comptroller and Auditor General of India, Report: *on Performance Audit on the issue of Licences and Allocation of 2G Spectrum*, (March, 2010).

2. Government of India, Administrative Reform Commission, Interim Report: *on the Problem of Redress of Citizen's Grievances* (Ministry of Law and Justice, 1966).
3. Government of India, Report: *Committee on Prevention of Corruption, (*Ministry of Law and Justice, 1964).
4. Government of Rajasthan, *Report of the Administrative Reforms Committee* (Ministry of Law and Justice, 1963).

(v) Webliography

Web References

1. A Brief time line of the Lokpal Bill, India, *available at:* http://www.prsindia.org/administrator/uploads/general/1302860449_Lok%20Pal%20Bill%20Timeline.pdf (Visited on March 02, 2013*),* see also Timeline: The Lokpals long walk to Law, India, *available at* : http://blogs.wsj.com/indiarealtime/2013/12/18/timeline-the-lokpals-long-walk-to-law/(Visited on March 03, 2013).
2. Constitutionality of section 4(1)(d) of the Lokpal and Lokayuktas Act under challenge before the high court of Kerala, India, *available at:* http://www.livelaw.in/constitutionality-section-41d-lokpal-lokayuktas-act-challenge-high-court-kerala/(Visited on March 27, 2014).
3. Corruption Perception Index, India, *available at*: http://www.transparency.org/country#IND (Visited on February 01, 2014).
4. Excluding PM from Lokpal unconstitutional, India, *available at:*http://indiacurrentaffairs.org/excluding-pm-from-lokpal-unconstitutional-prof-madabhushi-sridhar/ (Visited on March 27, 2014).
5. Gerald E. Caiden, "International Handbook of the Ombudsman" 2 *Country Surveys*, 180 (1983). *available at* http://www.livelaw.in/the-lokpal-and-lokayuktas-bill-2013-is-act-no-1-of-2014-will-new-section-8b2-of-

cvc-act-dilute-the-powers-of-cbi/(visited on 06/03/2014).

6. http://pib.nic.in/archieve/others/2005/hs01mar2k5.pdf (visited on February 27, 2014).
7. Human Development report shows worsening poverty in South Asia, India, *available at:*http://www.wsws.org/en/articles/1999/11/sasa-n29.html (Visited on April 11, 2014).
8. Issues related to the Lokpal Bill, Second Administrative Reform commission (2007), India, *available at* http://www.prsindia.org/administrator/uploads/general/1302082895_Issue%20Brief%20on%20Lok%20Pal%20Bil.pdf(Visited on February 6, 2014).
9. Issues related to the Lokpal Bill, national commission to review the working of the Constitution (2002), India, *availableat* : http://www.prsindia.org/administrator/uploads/general/1302082895_Issue%20Brief%20on%20Lok%20Pal%20Bil.pdf(Visited on February 5, 2014).
10. Lokpal and the Prime Minister, India, *available at*: http://www.thehindu.com/opinion/lead/lokpal-bill-and-the-prime-minister/article2148073.ece(Visited on March 26, 2014).
11. Lokpal:Constitutionality of Search Committee Rules, 2014 under challenge before the Supreme Court and Madras High Court, India, *available at:* http://www.livelaw.in/lokpal-constitutionality-search-committee-rules-2014-challenge-supreme-court-madras-high-court/(Visited on March 06, 2014).
12. Many advantages in Lokpal as a constitutional body, India, *available at:*https://indialawyers.wordpress.com/tag/rahul-gandhi/ (Visited on April 11, 2014).
13. National Common Minimum Programme of the Government of India, available at:
14. Will new section- 8B(2) of CVC Act dilute the powers of CBI?, India, *availbleat*: http://www.livelaw.in/the-lokpal-

and-lokayuktas-bill-2013-is-act-no-1-of-2014-will-new-section-8b2-of-cvc-act-dilute-the-powers-of-cbi/(Visited on March 06, 2014).

Websites

1. http://ncrb.nic.in/
2. www.findlaw.com
3. www.google.com
4. www.indiankanoon.com
5. www.legallyindia.com
6. www.ssrn.com

Index